HISTORY OF THE PUBLIC SCHOOL KINDERGARTEN IN NORTH CAROLINA

WITHDRAWN

By
Rebecca Murray

Meredith College

MSS Information Corporation
655 Madison Avenue, New York, N.Y. 10021

Library of Congress Cataloging in Publication Data

Murray, Rebecca.
  History of the public school kindergarten in North
Carolina

  Bibliography: p.
  1. Kindergartens — North Carolina — History. I. Title
LB1235.N8M87   372.21'8'09756   74-12132
ISBN 0-8422-0414-8

CONTENTS

CHAPTER I

INTRODUCTION

The kindergarten movement in the United States was
begun mostly through the efforts of individuals and financed
through private sources. The purposes and principles under-
lying the establishment and growth of the kindergarten in the
United States came by way of European influence.

The word kleinkinderbeschäftigungsanstalt (literally,
an institution for small children who are engaged in no
particular occupation) had been coined by a German teacher
named Friedrich Wilhelm Froebel (1782-1852). The term was
later reduced to "kindergarten." Froebel, often referred to
in the literature as the "father of the kindergarten," used
the word to express in exact terms his idea as to the way
children developed. To him, a kindergarten was a place where
children would be allowed to grow as naturally as flowers in
a garden.[1]

As a young man, Froebel had felt the influence of Johann
Heinrich Pestalozzi (1746-1827). Through personal contact with
Pestalozzi, he began to recognize the importance of the home
and environment to a child's education and the value of object
teaching. For several years Froebel taught at Pestalozzi's
Institute at Yverdon, Switzerland. This teaching experience
not only gave him the opportunity to observe and participate
in Pestalozzian method, but to formulate his own philosophy
about the education of the young.[2]

Froebel's ideas on early childhood education included
the use of "gifts" and "occupations" for the purpose of helping
children gain a sense of unity. The gifts were to lead a child
to the fundamental truths about the world and to provide creative
self-activity. The occupations were to provide a child with
the opportunity to control and change malleable materials and
to further and internalize the impressions formed by the gifts.
Froebel's gifts and occupations are described as follows:

GIFTS

SOLIDS

First gift: Six colored worsted balls about one inch and
              a half in diameter
Second gift: Wooden ball, cylinder, cube, one inch and a
              half in diameter
Third gift: Eight one-inch cubes--forming a two-inch cube
Fourth gift: Eight brick-shaped blocks, 2 x 1 x 1/2
Fifth gift: 27 one-inch cubes, three bisected, three quad-
              risected diagonally forming a three-inch cube
Sixth gift: 27 brick-shaped blocks, three bisected longi-
              tundinally, six bisected transversely

SURFACES

Seventh gift: Squares--entire and bisected
               Equilateral triangles--entire, half, thirds

LINES

Eighth gift: Straight--splints of various lengths
              Circular--metal or paper rings

POINTS

Ninth gift: Beans, lentils, seeds, pebbles

RECONSTRUCTION

Tenth gift: Softened peas or wax pellets and sharpened
             sticks or straw
             To reconstruct the surface and solid synthetically
             from the point

OCCUPATIONS

SOLiDS

Plastic clay, cardboard work, woodcarving

SURFACES

Paper folding, papercutting, parquetry, painting

LINES

Interlacing, intertwining, weaving, embroidery, drawing

POINTS

Stringing beads, perforating[3]

In 1837, Froebel opened his own school in Blankenburg,
Germany, thereby establishing the first kindergarten which
was based on the concept of unity. From 1837-1848, kindergartens and kindergarten training institutions continued to
grow throughout Europe. Since the Prussian Government deemed
kindergartens harmful to the interest of the state, however,
an edict went into effect in 1851 which prohibited any additional kindergartens from opening in that country. Many of
Froebel's students nevertheless retained his ideas and put
them into practice elsewhere.[4]

    Margarethe Meyer Schurz (1831-1876) and her family left
Prussia because of the failure of the Revolution of 1848.

After settling in Watertown, Wisconsin, Mrs. Schurz established
the first reported kindergarten in the United States. Her
kindergarten was organized in 1856 for the purpose of offering
such experience to her own two daughters and several cousins.[5]

The Froebelian influence on the education of the young
continued in America through a chance meeting between Margarethe
Schurz and Elizabeth Palmer Peabody (1804-1894). After a
conversation with Schurz, Peabody became interested in kindergarten principles and procedures. In an article published in
1882, Peabody described the conversation as follows:

"That little child of yours is a miracle--so child-like
and unconscious, and yet to wise and able, attracting and
ruling the children, who seem nothing short of enchanted."

"No miracle, but only brought up in a kindergarten,"
said Mrs. Schurz.

"A kindergarten! What is that?"

"A garden whose plants are human. Did you never hear
of Froebel?"

"No; who is he?"

"A greater discoverer in education than Pestalozzi. He
came to Hamburg in 1840, invited by Madame Johanna Goldschmidt
at the instigation of Diesterweg, who announced him to her as
a prophet. He opened lectures to mothers, and instructed
children's nurses and kindergartners by precept and exempli-
fication. All liberal people went to hear and see him; among
others, my sister, Madame Ronge, and myself; and I was so
fascinated I kept a journal-report of what he said to mothers
and did with the children."[6]

In 1860, in Boston, Massachusetts, Peabody opened the first
kindergarten for English-speaking children in the United States,
thereby launching a lifelong interest in promoting kindergartens
for all children in America.

The pre-first grade school concept was extended when the
first public school kindergarten was established through the
leadership of William T. Harris (1835-1909) and Susan E. Blow
(1843-1916) in St. Louis, Missouri, in 1873. Harris was Superintendent of Schools in St. Louis from 1868 to 1880, and in
1889 became U.S. Commissioner of Education. Blow volunteered
her time and services to direct the St. Louis kindergarten
and to instruct teachers in the methods of kindergarten work.[7]

Interest in early childhood education has grown and
over the years it has been generally recognized that the early
years are crucial ones in the lives of children. Concern for
children whose lives have been confined by a deprivation of
experiences for school success is evidenced by some of the
more recent federal programs. One result of the programs has
been that pre-first grade experiences are available to more
children than before, not just to those whose parents can
afford such services through private agencies. North Carolina
has been added to the list of states making an effort to provide

public kindergarten experiences for young children.

The purpose of this book was to examine the historical development of the kindergarten program in the public school system of North Carolina. In order to accomplish this purpose, emphasis was given to (1) ascertaining the legal provisions for the establishment of kindergartens in North Carolina; (2) reviewing the early private interests in schools for young children in North Carolina which served as a foundation for efforts to establish public schools for five-year-old children; (4) discovering each time kindergartens were established as a part of the public school system in North Carolina, and reporting information concerning the inclusion of the kindergarten; and (5) reporting information concerning the 1969 extension of the public school system to include kindergartens.

This study was concerned with the historical development of the kindergarten in the public school system of North Carolina. Facets of education related to five-year-old children in the state were examined in general, and specific attention was given to public programs for five-year-old children.

Early private efforts to establish kindergartens in North Carolina were studied as background information. Private efforts initiated after the introduction into the state of public kindergartens in Asheville in 1907, however, were not examined. No attempt was made to evaluate the kindergarten program as organized and implemented in 1969 by the State Department of Public Instruction, and only the first biennium (1969-1971) of the public kindergarten program was treated.

In 1968, the Governor's Study Commission recommended that the State of North Carolina provide kindergartens for five-year-olds on the same basis as educational programs were provided for students in grades 1-12. The initial step was to include 25 per cent of the five-year-olds in the program. Eight kindergartens, generally referred to as Early Childhood Demonstration Centers, were opened in 1969, and ten more in 1970. In 1970, 10.5 percent of the five-year-olds in North Carolina were enrolled in public kindergartens.[8] The projected plan is to include all five-year-olds in a kindergarten program by 1975-1977.[9]

The aforementioned Commission's recommendation and the kindergartens subsequently established were the culmination of much work and effort on the part of many private citizens and public officials of North Carolina. As early as 1878, Kemp Battle, President of the University of North Carolina, added significantly to early childhood education programs in North Carolina when he brought a specialist in kindergartens from New York City to teach kindergarten methods in the Normal School. The same year, Braxton Craven, first President of Trinity College, employed two experienced kindergartners from Washington, D. C., to offer courses in kindergarten training.

Early recognition by Battle and Craven of the necessity for educational experiences for children prior to the first grade seemed to provide the impetus for other expressions of interest in developing a public kindergarten program. Exemplifying the interest expressed were the maintenance of public kindergartens in the Asheville city schools from 1907 to 1930, and, twenty years later, the recommendation of the Superintendent of Public Instruction that kindergartens be included in the public school system of the entire state. More than sixty years after the establishment of the first public kindergartens in Asheville, Roanoke Rapids Graded School District recommended the inclusion of a kindergarten as a part of the public school p rogram. That kindergarten began in September, 1968.

With the Governor's Study Commission Report in 1968, and the opening of eighteen demonstration centers, North Carolina laid the foundation for a state—wide kindergarten program. Little doubt exists that such a program will have a significant positive effect on the status of education in North Carolina. Some indicate that efforts to provide enriched opportunities in the lives of young children may help to circumvent behavioral programs and reduce the school drop—out rate.

The study of the development of the public kindergarten in North Carolina will provide information that heretofore has been in records not readily available. The information gained from the records has been compiled in one source, and may contribute to an understanding of the interest in the growth and development of public kindergartens in North Carolina. Recognition was also given to the accomplishments of various persons in the state who influenced the emphasis placed on schools for pre-first grade children. It is hoped that the findings of this book will aid in planning for the future educational needs of the state.

CHAPTER II

EFFORTS TO ESTABLISH KINDERGARTENS

PRIOR TO 1940

The history of education in North Carolina indicates that the people have desired schooling for young children and have endeavored to establish ways to realize this goal. As early as 1840, "An Act for the establishment and better regulation of Common Schools" was passed by the General Assembly of the state. According to this law, all white children under the age of twenty-one would be permitted to attend school and would be allowed to receive instruction.[1] Taken at face value, all white five-year-olds in North Carolina would have had the opportunity to attend school.

Provision was made in the legislative session of 1923 for establishing kindergartens at public expense. The voters in any school district could vote in favor of a special tax to provide physical facilities, equipment, and maintenance of a kindergarten department. The age of the children who could attend the kindergartens was to be "not more than six years of age."[2]

The Asheville city schools maintained public kindergartens from 1907 to 1930, as did the Washington public schools from 1910 to 1915. The kindergartens in the Asheville schools were the first public ones in session in North Carolina prior to 1940. According to a 1907 law, children as young as three years of age were permitted to go to school in Asheville.[3] Apparently no legal arrangements were made in connection with the Washington public kindergartens.

For the school year 1955-56 and for each year thereafter, school laws stated that in order to attend school children must have passed the sixth anniversary of their birth before October 1 of the year in which they would enroll in school.[4] The law was not changed until 1969, when the North Carolina General Assembly provided kindergartens that would be financed through public funds.

Generally speaking, more interest was expressed in private efforts to establish kindergartens in the state prior to 1940 than in public efforts. Since the main emphasis of this study is the historical development of the public kindergarten, private efforts to establish schools for young children will be treated in this chapter only for the period prior to the establishment of the public kindergartens in Asheville.

Early private schools in North Carolina were called
Infant Schools, and they provided private instruction to
children from ages two to five. In the 1880's, several
institutions provided training for teachers who were interested in pursuing careers in kindergarten teaching.

Infant Schools . Apparently one of the earliest types
of schools to offer formal instruction to young children in
North Carolina was the Infant School. Infant Schools were
private schools and were open to children whose parents could
afford to pay for the services.

Probably the Infant School idea was first advocated
by Johann Amos Comenius (1592-1670). The emphasis in his
schools for young children was on food, fresh air, sleep,
and exercise for the purpose of developing a body that was
fit for the habitation of the soul.[5] About 150 years later,
a Frenchman, Jean Frédéric Oberlin (1740-1826), originated
the salles d'hospitalité (literally, a waiting room in a
hospital), which became salles d'asile (literally, a room
for refuge), and later became known as écoles maternelles
(literally, motherly schools), when the schools were incorporated into the public school system of France. The
object of Oberlin's school was to provide physical exercise
and moral training for children. In Germany, similar schools
were called Kleinkinderbewahranstalten (literally, an institution
for the care of small children).[6]

Infant Schools were provided for children who worked in
the mills owned by Robert Owen (1771-1858), the Welsh philan-
thropist. [7] Owen seemed interested in the young children who
had been apprenticed to him, and set up a school for these
children that emphasized health and physical exercise rather
than academic achievement. A few years later, similar schools,
which emphasized informal education for young children, were
established in the United States.[8]

The first Infant School in the United States was established
in Boston in 1818.[9] This school, as well as schools that sprang
up in other places in the United States, tended to be more formal
than the schools developed by Owen. As Infant Schools were
more generally adopted in the United States, each school was
established in such a way as to meet the needs of children in
a given locality.[10]

According to several newspaper articles, Infant Schools
were established in North Carolina during the 1830's, and
apparently each school was autonomous as to the program provided
for young children. An article in the Raleigh Register of
September 23, 1830, for example, described an Infant School
which had recently opened in Raleigh. This school for young
children was directed by a woman unnamed in the article, but
who was described as "a lady of character, experience, and

tenderness. . ."[11] It was stated that the lessons given to the children were simple at first, in order not to fatigue the mind, but progressively the lessons became more difficult, individually structured to suit the needs of each child. The school was recommended to parents as a place to prepare children for "higher schools."[12] Although instruction was at the core of the school, the article noted that the school could also serve the purpose of keeping children out of mischief.[13]

An Infant School in Fayetteville was maintained in 1832 by a Mrs. Bethune. Mrs. Bethune had an "Assistant Instructress" and a servant to aid in the work with children. The school was for children from ages two to eight. Mrs. Bethune thought that a large number of children should be taught at one time in order to provide more children with instruction. The instruction cost 12-1/2 cents a week.[14]

In 1842, a Mrs. Peat, "an amiable Instructress," directed an Infant School in Raleigh. According to an article in the North Carolina Standard, early education reaped positive rewards: "Who sends a child to the Infant School is repaid a hundred fold for the trifling expense incurred."[15]

Infant Schools that had been established in various cities and towns in the United States seemed to lose identity as the primary grades of the common schools became more prevalent.[16]

Normal College, Randolph County, 1850-1855. Normal College in Randolph County was organized for the purpose of instructing teachers. The State Legislature granted the College the authority to award teaching certificates to the graduates and the certificates would be valid anywhere in North Carolina.[17]

The activities of Normal College were under the direction of Dr. Braxton Craven, who considered teaching a "great profession." In the 1851-52 Catalogue of Normal College, Randolph County, North Carolina, Craven wrote: "Teaching is a great profession, it is now a profitable business; a splendid theatre of usefulness is open, and good actors are in great demand."[18] In the 1852-53 Catalogue, Craven emphasized the importance of children having excellent instruction during their early years. He noted: "Parents who desire giving their sons a liberal education, should be quite as careful in selecting their primary teachers as in determining the college at which they shall finish their studies."[19] In the same Catalogue, Craven continued his support of early education by stating that "we are under many obligations, for every College owes its grade in scholarship and the intellectual development of its graduates very materially, to the character of the primary instruction among its patrons."[20]

Throughout the five-year period that Normal College remained a teacher training institution, its students were able to practice their teaching skills in a model school for young children. Craven described the school as follows: "(A) Model School of small children; in this school, the Normal candidates practice; here, under the inspection of the President, they are drilled

in all the minutiae of governing and teaching. . . ."21
Neither the Normal College catalogues nor the Craven papers
revealed the age of the children who attended the Model
School.

Trinity College Normal School, 1856. In 1856, Normal
College of Randolph County became affiliated with the North
Carolina Methodist Conference and was renamed Trinity College.
Craven was retained as President of the College and he continued
to express an interest in the education of young children.
In the February 6, 1878, issue of the Raleigh Christian
Advocate, Craven announced plans to conduct a normal school
that would be in session during the summer.22

Two months later, in the Raleigh Christian Advocate,
Craven announced that the Normal School was to begin June 20,
1878, and would continue for four weeks. He also noted that
an outstanding feature of the school would be the absence of
fees for instruction. The only cost to a student would be
for room and board, at the rate of $1.50 to $2.50 per week.
Living arrangements for all persons on campus were to be
satisfactory, and the ladies were to receive accommodations
described as "abundant." Craven encouraged teachers and those
who wanted to teach, and "all who feel an interest in the
subject" to attend the school.23 After the Normal School had
begun, Craven reported that it was a success. He stated that
a tone of plesantness prevailed, "but the work is decisive,
earnest and somewhat heavy."24

Connected with the summer session was a school composed
of twenty kindergarten children. The purpose of this school
was to allow the theories and skills of teaching to be tested.
According to Craven, the school was regarded as "one of the
most interesting and profitable exercises of the School."25

Apparently Craven recognized the value of bringing
consultants to the summer session for the purpose of working
with those persons interested in kindergarten work. In an
announcement in the Raleigh Christian Advocate of July 24, 1878,
Craven stated that Mrs. Louise Pollock and her daughter, Susie
Pollock, from Washington, D.C., would soon arrive to offer
kindergarten instruction.26 Louise Pollock, a native of Prussia,
was influenced by a book entitled Moral Culture in Infancy and
and Kindergarten Guide, written by Elizabeth Peabody and her
sister, Mary Mann, in 1863. Louise Pollock established a
kindergarten in West Newton, Massachusetts, in 1864. Later,
in the 1870's and 1880's, she maintained the National Kindergarten and Primary School of Washington, D.C. Susie Pollock is
credited with opening the first kindergarten in Washington,
D.C., in 1870.27

Concerning the credentials of the Pollocks, Craven wrote:
"They are not simply teachers of object lessons, as are most of
those who profess to be teachers in this department, but are
thorough Kindergartners, graduates from the best School in Prussia,
and highly accomplished."28

An examination of Trinity College catalogues by the researcher yielded no evidence that the Pollocks returned to Trinity after 1878, nor that the College offered kindergarten instruction after that date.

Peace Institute Kindergarten, 1879-1889. Peace Institute, in Raleigh, was established in 1857 by the First Presbyterian Church of that city. In 1872, the Reverend Robert Burwell became the principal of Peace Institute and was assisted in his duties by his son, John.[29] Seven years after becoming principal, Burwell introduced a kindergarten department in the Institute, and children from the Raleigh area were enrolled. One of the purposes of the kindergarten was to allow Peace Institute students to practice their teaching skills.[30]

Julia W. Stephenson, one of the students in Emily Coe's 1878 class at the University of North Carolina, was named principal of the primary and kindergarten department in 1879 at Peace Institute. Stephenson was assisted in her duties by Jennie Faison, who was also a student of Coe's.[31] The kindergarten was housed in a structure set apart from the main building, and measured 40 x 25 feet. In the building were "desks and chairs of the latest and most improved pattern" that had been personally constructed by Burwell.[32] At the time of the writing of this book some of the desks remain in the Administration Building at Peace College.

The children were instructed in spelling, arithmetic, vocal music, and art. The Catalogue of 1880 noted: "The pupils receive instruction according to the approved Kindergarten methods, which seem destined to greatly modify and improve the ordinary plans of Primary Instruction."[33] The thirty-four pupils enrolled in the first kindergarten at Peace Institute in 1879 were taught for the sum of $15 per term.[34]

From 1879 until 1889, the kindergarten department continued to accept young children.[35] In 1886, a Normal Department, directed by Charles D. McIver, was established for those persons who wanted to teach, and the kindergarten was used by students to practice skills in teaching.[36] According to the catalogues, the kindergarten was discontinued at Peace Institute in 1889, but the primary department continued to accept students between the ages of eight and twelve.[37]

St. Paul's School, 1858-1938. One of the private efforts in North Carolina to perpetuate the growth and interest in kindergartens was St. Paul's School, in Beaufort. The first effort to establish the Episcopal school was begun in 1858. The person involved in the planning and operation of the school included the rector of the parish and a young woman named Sallie Pasteur, who was a descendant of Louis Pasteur. The school was maintained until 1867.[38]

An effort to reëstablish St. Paul's School was made under the direction of Nannie Geffroy. Mary Anna Geffroy, née Davis, was born July 21, 1865, the daughter of James C. and Sallie Pasteur Davis. She became known as Nannie and the nickname remained with her throughout her life. In 1885, Nannie Davis married M. R. Geffroy.[39]

The Episcopal school was established for the purpose of promoting Christian principles in boys and girls. The school enrolled students from kindergarten through high school, and efforts were made to provide the children and young people with experiences that would influence their social, intellectual, and spiritual lives.[40]

On November 1, 1900, the cornerstone of St. Paul's School was laid and shortly thereafter the three-story building was completed. The kindergarten section of the school was located on the third floor, and the cost for each child enrolled in the kindergarten was $1.00 per month.[41]

Nannie Geffroy continued to provide educational opportunities to many children in Beaufort until her death on December 20, 1936. Several teachers in the school attempted to continue St. Paul's, but their endeavors failed and the school closed in 1938.[42]

For at least one year, a training school for kindergarten teachers was maintained by St. Paul's School. Apparently only one catalogue exists that reveals any information about the training school.[43] In the catalogue of 1909-1910, the aim of the training school was expressed as follows:

> The aim of the training school is to give a special training to all women who have the care of young children and to others who wish to be aided by thorough discipline and increased insight which the study of the Kindergarten gives; and to prepare young women to take positions as principals of Kindergartens.[44]

In connection with the training school there was a kindergarten where students were provided the opportunity to observe methods of teaching kindergarten children and to put their teaching skills into practice. Each student in the school was required to enroll in prescribed courses for a two-year period. During both years of study students were required to work in the kindergarten from 9:00 A.M. to 12:00 noon, five days a week, and to go to class from 2:00 to 3:30 in the afternoon.[45]

Upon completion of the work at the St. Paul's training school, each student was entitled to a diploma and was deemed qualified to become a principal or a teacher in a kindergarten.[46]

The requirements for the diploma included working in the kindergarten at the school and completing course requirements consisting of the study of the kindergarten, theory and practice, theory of education, psychology, physics, physiology, history, music, literature, and nature study.[47]

Caroline Carrow, Director of the "practice kindergarten," also taught the courses in the theory of kindergarten, theory of education, psychology, physics, physiology, and nature study. According to the Catalogue, other faculty memebers were Ellen V. Apperson, who taught history; Mary T. Lassiter, who gave instruction in music; and Edward T. Hills, who provided the courses in literature.[48]

Caroline Carrow was listed in the Catalogue as the Director of the Kindergarten, but no other personnel connected with the kindergarten per se were mentioned. Although Margaret Johnson was not mentioned in the Catalogue, she taught kindergarten courses at the University of North Carolina from 1901 to 1905 and was probably one of the kindergartners working with the students in the training school.[49]

For each student, tuition at St. Paul's Training School was $50 per year. In addition, board, fuel, and lights were provided at a cost of $10 to $20 per month. For students who needed financial assistance in order to attend the school, "loan scholarships" which could be repaid after a student had graduated were available.[50]

Privately owned mills. In the Biennial Report of the Superintendent of Public Instruction, 1912-1914, a recommendation was made that supported the protection of women and children working in factories. Specifically, the recommendation stated:

> For the protection of childhood and womanhood, the foundation upon which our whole civilization rests, I urgently recommended (sic) improving and enlarging the present laws regulating the labor of children and women in the factories and the extension, and the extension (sic) of these laws to include all companies, corporations and individuals employing children and women. I recommend also the establishment of an efficient system of State inspection for the enforcement of such laws. I refrain from specific recommendations at this time awaiting the recommendations of the North Carolina Child Labor Committee, the Conference for Social Service, and other organizations that are making a special study of this subject, and I shall heartily cooperate with such organizations in recommending and securing the enactment and enforcement of any reasonable laws for the better protection of childhood and womanhood.[51]

Since women were working in industry, several mills operated kindergartens for the children of their employees. In 1912, kindergartens were provided by private mills in the cities of Greensboro, Lumberton, and Wilmington.[52] An examination of the Reports of the Superintendent of Public Instruction and Kindergartens in the United States published by the Bureau of Education did not reveal additional mill schools for kindergarten children in North Carolina.

Proximity Manufacturing Company, in Greensboro, offered a kindergarten for the children of the workers in the company. Sixty-one children were enrolled in the kindergarten, and the average daily attendance was forty-five children. The kindergarten was operated 180 days per years, with three teachers employed to work with the children. The salary paid to the teachers was $480 per year.[53]

In Lumberton, thirty-five children attended kindergarten at the Jennings Cotton Mill. The average daily attendance was thirty children, and the kindergarten was in session 160 days each year. One teacher was in charge of the children, and she was paid $320 per year for her services.[54]

The Delgodo Mills in Wilmington provided a kindergarten for fifty children, with an average daily attendance of thirty. No data were available concerning the number of days the kindergarten operated per year nor the amount of money paid to the two teachers employed by the Mills.[55]

According to Cook's study published in 1925, mill employees sent their children to school at an earlier age than six for two reasons. First, the children were left unattended because both the father and the mother worked in the mill, and, second, since there was nothing for the children to do at home alone, school was deemed the best place for them. In his study, Cook recommended that a well-organized kindergarten be available in the mills so that the young children might gain from the educational opportunity.[56]

Public Interest in Schools for Young Children

The first public efforts supported by public funds to establish kindergartens occurred through the course offerings at the University of North Carolina Normal School. The first session that provided kindergarten instruction was in 1878, and Emily Coe was employed to teach the course. Coe was also employed by the Asheville State Normal School, and gave kindergarten instruction to teachers attending the summer session of 1885.

Asheville was the first school district in North Carolina to finance kindergartens through public money prior to 1940. The kindergartens were begun in 1907 and were maintained by the Asheville school system until 1930, when Attorney General Dennis Brummitt ruled the schools illegal because there had been no vote of the people. The public schools of the City of Washington also provided a kindergarten from 1910 to 1915.

The lack of kindergartens in North Carolina was a source of concern for those at a national level who were interested in the establishment of kindergartens in all states. Expressions from out-of-state to the Superintendent of Public Instruction in North Carolina indicate a national interest in the plans of North Carolina to provide greater educational opportunities for young children in the state. Within the state, the North Carolina Congress of Parents and Teachers, one year after its organization in 1919, called for support of the kindergarten as a part of the public school system of North Carolina.

University of North Carolina Normal School, 1878-1905. In 1878, the summer session of the Normal School at the University of North Carolina at Chapel Hill opened on June 18.[57] The State of North Carolina encouraged the summer session by granting $500 to assist teachers desiring to attend the school. Eighty-three teachers received aid, and railroad and steamboat companies in the state reduced their fares to allow teachers to travel to Chapel Hill at a less expensive rate.[58]

Kemp Battle, President of the University, felt that instruction in kindergarten work should be made a part of the curriculum offered during the summer session. He wrote: "So much attention had been given in recent years to the training of children it was thought best to employ an instructor in the Kindergarten system."[59] The person Battle obtained was Emily M. Coe, of New York City. Coe had established her own kindergarten, the American Kindergarten, in New York City, in 1860.[60] At the University of North Carolina, Coe offered a class in kindergarten instruction, and sixteen teachers enrolled.[61] The teachers, under Coe's direction, worked with "53 children of various ages" in order to gain firsthand experience in the instruction of young children.[62] On July 23, the day before final exercises of the 1878 session, the kindergarten children gave a presentation to the school and "exhibited the perfection of their training under Miss Coe and her coadjutors."[63]

In addition to her regular duties as kindergarten instructor, Coe presented a lecture to the entire Normal School.[64] Her topic was on form and color, and Battle described the lecture by stating that "Miss Coe, in the graceful style for which women are conspicuous, lectured on 'Color and Form.'"[65] According to Battle, Coe's work at the 1878 summer session, beginning two days before the Trinity College session, was the introduction of kindergarten instruction into North Carolina.[66]

The 1879 Normal School opened on June 17 and continued for five weeks.[67] President Battle again obtained Coe to offer kindergarten instruction. Battle stated:

> Miss Coe may be considered the introducer into
> North Carolina of Kindergarten instruction. She was
> not only extremely skillful with her class of children
> but formed an advanced class of teachers and imparted
> the system to them. To those of us who remembered how
> odious the monotony and confinement of school were to
> us in our boyhood it was a marvel to see children of
> all ages eager for Miss Coe's school to begin and

regretful of its ending.[68]

Again, Coe presented a lecture to the whole Normal School. Her topic on this occasion was "The Teacher's Work: Its Rewards."[69]

The 1880 five-week Normal School summer session, which opened June 24, continued to offer instruction in kindergarten work. Louise Pollock and her daughter, Susie Pollock, of Washington, D. C., were the teachers, and Jane Long, of New York City, was the teacher in the Model School.[70] Instruction in kindergarten work covered the organization and management of kindergartens, methods of teaching kindergarten, and instruction to mothers about teaching their own children.[71]

In the sessions of 1881 and 1882, instruction in kindergarten work continued. Jane Long remained in North Carolina, and was the teacher of the model class for both summer sessions.[72] Changes were made in the 1883 summer session. According to the Catalogue of 1882-84, Long was replaced by Mary O. Humphrey, of Goldsboro. Humphrey's work seemed to encompass the early school years, since her title was "teacher of Model Primary Class."[73]

Instruction in kindergarten was not listed in the catalogues from 1886 to 1897. In the summer of 1898, kindergarten courses were offered by Mary Shakelford MacRae.[74] MacRae taught courses entitled "Practical Course," "Gifts and Occupations," and "Stories and Games."[75] After the 1898 session, courses in kindergarten teaching were not offered at the University of North Carolina again until 1901.[76] In 1901, Margaret A. Johnson, of the Beaufort Kindergarten Training School, offered the kindergarten courses.[77] Johnson retained her position with the University of North Carolina summer sessions until 1905. A review of the Minutes of the Board of Trustees of the University of North Carolina from 1878 to 1905 did not reveal any information concerning the Normal School faculty during those years or why kindergarten instruction was discontinued in 1905.

Other state-funded institutions. In addition to kindergarten instruction provided at public expense at the University of North Carolina Normal School, four other state-supported teacher training institutions offered kindergarten work for a period of time. One of the schools was located in Asheville, one in Franklin, one in Newton, and one in Washington.

According to an article in the North Carolina Educational Journal dated August 15, 1881, the kindergarten department of the Normal School at Franklin, established that year under the direction of Nettie Marshall, a student in Miss Coe's class at UNC in 1878, was "one of the most interesting and instructive features of the School."[78] As a part of the activities of the Normal School at Newton, a kindergarten was established in 1881 and at least seventy children were enrolled.[79] Jane C. Wade, from Columbia, South Carolina, was employed to conduct the kindergarten.

In 1885, the Asheville State Normal School opened, and

during the summer session of 1886, according to the Biennial
Report of the Superintendent of Public Instruction, Emily Coe
gave instruction in kindergarten teaching.[80] In 1888, the
Report noted that Mamie Hall, from Illinois, offered courses in
kindergarten and drawing at the Washington Normal School.[81] The
Report of the Superintendent gave no indication that kindergarten
instruction was offered at any of the state-supported normal
institutions which had been specifically established for black
students, during the period prior to 1940.

A kindergarten program was first established at the North
Carolina Institute for the Deaf and Dumb and the Blind in 1892.
According to the Report of the Institute for 1892-1894, the aim
of the kindergarten program was as follows: "To develop both
the mind and body of the children in accordance with natural
laws. Blind children need such development even more than sighted
children do."[82] The kindergarten program, under the direction
of Anna T. Jones, provided a schedule of four and one-half hours
daily for the children to develop in accordance with the aim of
the program.[83]

The kindergarten program continued each year thereafter at
the North Carolina Institute for the Deaf and Dumb and the Blind.
In the 1902-1904 Report, emphasis was placed on the fact that
the program was a part of the public school system of the state,
although the program was only for the handicapped children
attending the school.[84] The school has continued to maintain
a kindergarten program since 1892 although the program was renamed in 1968 and was called "Beginners Class." The present
principal, John Calloway, stated that the school is considering
a restructuring of the Beginners Class so that it will be more
in line with the current organizational patterns of kindergarten
programs at the state level.[85]

Kindergartens in the Public Schools in the State

The first public school kindergarten program in North
Carolina was in Asheville. The only other public school
kindergarten program in the state prior to 1940 was operated by
the Washington public schools.

Asheville City Schools kindergartens. The Asheville Free
Kindergarten Association, organized in 1889, supported and maintained three private kindergartens in the city but wanted to
turn them over to the public school system.[86] Due to financial
difficulties, the Free Kindergarten Association expressed the
willingness to present all buildings, lands, and school equipment as a gift to the Asheville City Schools.[87]

An act to authorize the school committee of the Asheville
City Schools to take control of the kindergartens was passed
by the General Assembly of North Carolina on February 23, 1907.[88]
Legally, the pupils in the kindergartens were to be considered
a part of the school population, and children between the ages

of three and five would be allowed to attend kindergarten.[89]
The Asheville School Committee voted on June 21, 1907, to take
charge of the kindergartens beginning September, 1907.[90]
Superintendent R. S. Tighe reported that the property acquired
from the Asheville Free Kindergarten Association included the
Sara Garrison building, equipment, and lot on East Street; the
Ann Hubbard building, equipment, and lot on Louie Street; and
the equipment in the Riverside Club building in the Asheville
Cotton Mill.[91]

By 1910, the Asheville schools were maintinaing four
kindergartens. One hundred ninety-one children were enrolled
in the Asheville kindergartens: fifty-four at the Orange
Street School, fifty at the East Street School, forty-eight
at the Park Avenue School, and thirty-nine at the Murray School
on Tiernan Street.[92] By 1913, the Ashland Street School had
been added to the list of those offering public school kindergartens. In 1929, Edmonds reported that the Asheville City
Schools operated ten kindergartens.[93]

The Minutes of the School Committee of Asheville, July 9,
1909, to July 6, 1913, revealed the names of the persons employed
to teach in the kindergartens and the salary schedule. In 1913,
H. Ethel Ray taught at the Orange Street School and received
$39 per month for her services; Gussie Smith taught at the
Ashland Avenue School and received $25 per month; Carrie Wagner
taught at the Park Avenue School and was paid $35 per month;
Hattie M. Scott taught at the Murray School and was paid $39 per
month; and Alice Stockton, at the East Street School, received
$32.50 per month.[94]

The children enrolled in the kindergartens did not attend
school for the same number of days as children in other grades.
The number of days the kindergarten children went to school and
the number of days the other children went to school are set
forth below:

Year	Number of Days	
	Kindergarten Children	Other Children
1908	150	182
1909	150	190
1910	150	190
1911	170	190[95]

At the regular meeting of the School Committee on March 7, 1910,
Superintendent Tighe suggested that the kindergarten term be
increased to nine months. The suggestion was not accepted because
of a lack of funds to pay for the additional time.[96]

The kindergartens remained a part of the public school system
of Asheville until 1930. At that time, the Attorney General of
North Carolina, Dennis Brummitt, rendered an opinion that the

operation and maintenance of kindergartens in Asheville was illegal because the people of the district had not voted for kindergartens.[97] The announcement concerning the termination of the kindergartens was made by Brummitt at City Hall in Asheville in late April, 1930.[98]

A search of Brummitt's papers in the Department of Archives and History did not reveal how the Asheville kindergarten situation was brought to the attention of the Attorney General. Conversations with Adrian Newton, Clerk of the North Carolina Supreme Court, and Raymond Taylor, Marshal and Librarian of the Supreme Court, indicated that no sources were available which would shed light on such information.[99] The termination of the kindergartens did, however, develop into a court case, Posey et al. v. Board of Education of Buncombe County et al., in an attempt to have the kindergartens reopened in the Asheville school system.[100]

The issue of the case was whether or not the Board of Education had the right to discontinue the kindergartens. The resolution of this issue depended essentially on the statutory interpretation of the pertinent legislation and on whether the kindergartens had in fact become a part of the public school system.[101]

The lower court held that the kindergartens were not a part of the public school system and that the power of the Board of Education to maintain the schools was a discretionary power. The Board of Education therefore had the right to discontinue the kindergartens.[102]

The Supreme Court of North Carolina reversed the decision of the lower court. The Supreme Court reasoned that the provisions of the statutes relative to the maintenance and operation of the kindergartens were mandatory. Also, those provisions had not been repealed or modified since 1907.[103] The Court concluded that at all times since the 1907 Act the kindergartens had been maintained as a part of the public school system of the City of Asheville. Based on such reasoning, the Court stated:

> (I)f the defendants have the power to maintain and operate kindergarten schools as part of the public school system of the city of Asheville, it is manifest, we think, that it is their duty to exercise the power, in good faith, and in accordance with the legislative will, clearly and plainly expressed in the statutes applicable to said schools.[104]

The Supreme Court decision discussed an issue in the case which had not been treated by the lower court, that of whether or not the General Assembly of North Carolina had the power to require the Board of Education to maintain schools for children below the age of six. The Court held that as long as there were funds available for the support of the kindergartens, the General Assembly had the power to require the operation and maintenance of the kindergartens. The Court, however, qualified the ruling by stating that if an additional tax was required to maintain the kindergartens, then the schools could be established only with the approval of the voters in the district.[105]

According to The History of the Kindergarten Movement of the Southeastern States, published in 1939 by the Association for Childhood Education, the Asheville kindergartens were re-opened in accordance with the Supreme Court decision, but only for one year because of financial problems that occurred.[106]

Washington public schools kindergartens. In May, 1909, two members of the Washington Public Schools Board of School Trustees, "Messrs. Kugler and Phillips," and Superintendent of Schools N. C. Newbold formed a committee "to make careful estimates of the receipts and disbursements for the next year, and to submit a general plan for the schools for the coming session."[107] Part of the general plan consisted of a new grade to be called 1C. The purpose of 1C was to combine kindergarten and the primary grades by allowing children who would be five years old in September to come to school.[108]

According to the October, 1910, issue of North Carolina Education, the kindergarten opened September 19 with an enrollment of 51 children. The kindergarten was directed by Mary E. Wright, a "trained kindergartner," who was assisted by Mary Lillian Ellsworth. In the article, the kindergarten was described as follows:

> We have a large, sunny room on the ground floor of the Public School building, a good supply of kindergarten materials, the use of a piano, and, so far, have had the interest and co-operation of the Superintendent of Schools, the School Board, the patrons and the town as a whole.[109]

The Report of the Superintendent, July 1, 1909-June 30, 1910, mentioned that the kindergarten that had begun in the school in 1910 had been a "decided success."[110] The Superintendent reported that the enrollment in September was approximately fifty children, and that the total number enrolled during the year was seventy. The Superintendent also noted that in January, 1911, several children in the kindergarten were promoted to the first grade.[111]

At the time the kindergarten was established in 1910, several other "new" departments were also added to the Washington schools, including domestic science and manual training. On May 26, 1915, the Board of School Trustees of Washington "decided to abolish the Kindergarten as part of the Public Schools and establish Domestic Science instead."[112]

23

The North Carolina Kindergarten Association and the North Carolina Congress of Parents and Teachers were two school-related organizations in the state that expressed interest in schools for young children. Both groups provided information to their members concerning kindergarten education, and both seemed to realize the significance of public kindergartens for North Carolina.

North Carolina Kindergarten Association. The North Carolina Kindergarten Association, a division of the North Carolina Teachers Assembly, apparently was not a strong organization. There are records, however, of several annual meetings.

The first program of the North Carolina Teachers Assembly to mention a kindergarten section was in 1904. Margaret Johnson and Mrs. A. P. Robinson were the leaders of the kindergarten section, and topics for discussion included:

What May We as Teachers Do to Extend Kindergarten Work?
The Relation Between Primary and Kindergarten Work
The First Three Months of School
The Importance of an Effective Organization of Primary Workers and How It May Be Secured[113]

Although meetings concerning kindergarten education had been held at the North Carolina Teachers Assembly since 1904, the North Carolina Kindergarten Association was not formally organized until 1912.[114] During the 1912 annual meeting of the NCTA, a group of twenty-two persons interested in kindergarten work became the charter members of the North Carolina Kindergarten Association. The main discussion for that first meeting was about Montessori and her work with young children. Annie E. George, President of the Montessori American Committee and the only American to have graduated from the Montessori school in Rome, was the speaker.[115]

Enough interest was being generated about kindergartens in North Carolina during the years 1910 and 1912 that a column entitled "Our Kindergarten Exchange" was a regular feature in North Carolina Education for several months during that period.[116] The column was composed of an exchange of various ideas and activities appropriate for kindergarten children.

In 1913, the meeting of the kindergarten association was scheduled for Thanksgiving Day. Hattie M. Scott, a teacher in one of the Asheville public kindergartens, was in charge of the program for the meeting, and in connection with the planning corresponded several times with E. E. Sams, Executive Secretary of the North Carolina Teachers Assembly. Sams needed the program prior to the meeting in 1913 for the purpose of sending out advance notice and advertising material.[117]

The original program proposed by Miss Scott listed the U.S.

Commissioner of Education, P.P. Claxton, as one of the speakers. Claxton was to speak on "The Kindergarten as Part of Our School System."[118] Later, Scott was informed that Claxton would be unable to attend the meeting. The final program consisted of a speech presented by Bertha Payne Newell on "The Influence of Montessori on the Kindergarten"; story-telling techniques by Richard Wyche, editor of Story Teller's Magazine; games and folk dances led by Scott and Newell; "Manual Training in the Kindergarten" by Ella Victoria Dobbs of the University of Missouri; and ten-minute "round table talks" by four primary and kindergarten teachers attending the meeting. In addition to the speeches and discussions, children's work from several kindergartens in the state was displayed.[119]

The 1915 meeting of the North Carolina Teachers Assembly was held in Raleigh. North Carolina Education reported that the kindergarten section of the Assembly was to meet and that the group would hear addresses given by Miss Brochhausen, from Indianapolis, Indiana, and Miss Cobb, from Edinboro, Pennsylvania.[120]

In March, 1923, Mary Leeper, representing the North Carolina Kindergarten Association, wrote a letter to the editor of North Carolina Education requesting that a page be devoted in each issue of the journal to kindergarten interests in North Carolina.[121] Leeper's request was granted, and beginning in the May, 1923, issue of North Carolina Education a section appeared entitled "Kindergarten Department." The articles in the section included announcements of NCKA meetings, health information that would be useful in working with kindergarten children, and a general exchange of ideas concerning work with young children.[122] The "Kindergarten Department" continued to be a regular feature of North Carolina Education until mid-summer, 1924.

Lucy Gage, of the George Peabody Institute, was engaged to present the main address to the meeting of the Association in March, 1924. Gage's interest in unifying kindergarten and first grade was expressed in her topic, "The Kindergarten as the First Step in Elementary Education."[123]

North Carolina Congress of Parents and Teachers. Since its beginning in 1919, the North Carolina Congress of Parents and Teachers has expressed interest in public kindergartens for North Carolina. That same year the organization was establishing various committees to function in the interest of education in the state, and one of the committees was designated as "Kindergarten extension."[124] Reports of the North Carolina Congress did not, however, state what the duties of the committee would be.

In 1920 the first resolution passed by the North Carolina Congress concerning kindergartens called for the kindergarten program for four- and five-year-olds in the state to be incorporated into the public schools "at the earliest possible moment."[125] The Congress has continued its stand for public

25

kindergartens throughout the years.

On April 3, 1924, the Board of Managers of the North Carolina Congress of Parents and Teachers passed a motion that created a department of kindergarten work.[126] In her 1937 report, Mrs. W. L. Wharton, chairman of the kindergarten department, noted that the public needed to be educated to the importance of kindergarten training in the lives of children, and that work on behalf of establishing kindergartens in schools with a high rate of first grade failures should be encouraged.[127]

Interest in Kindergartens in North Carolina from the National Level

Interest at the national level concerning kindergartens tended to increase year by year. Records reviewed at the North Carolina Department of Archives and History concerning the development of the kindergarten program in North Carolina indicated that at least two specialists in kindergarten education encouraged State Superintendent E. C. Brooks to consider public kindergartens for North Carolina.

Nina C. Vandewalker, Specialist in Kindergarten Education in the Bureau of Education in Washington, D. C., wrote to Dr. Brooks on June 21, 1921. In her letter, Vandewalker noted that the status of kindergartens varied in different states and that she hoped that North Carolina would become one of the states to realize growth in kindergarten education for young children.[128] Apparently Vandewalker wrote to Brooks as a part of her regular duties in her position as an education specialist in the Department of Interior.

Since the main objective of the National Kindergarten Association was "to have kindergartens provided for all of the Nation's children," the Corresponding Secretary of the organization took the opportunity to encourage Dr. Brooks to plan for kindergartens in the state. In a letter dated July 14, 1921, Bessie Locke noted that she had read an article by Brooks concerning a proposal to erect new school buildings in the state. Locke expressed the hope that such new buildings would all contain kindergarten classrooms. Locke also offered to furnish, without cost if necessary, leaflets that would explain the work and efforts of the National Kindergarten Association toward establishing kindergartens for all children in the nation.[129] Brooks's secretary replied to Locke's letter by writing: "Dear Madam:- I am requested by Dr. Brooks to thank you for your letter of July 14th."[130]

Kindergarten, State Normal and Industrial School, Greensboro

The State Normal and Industrial School was established in 1891 by an act of the North Carolina General Assembly.[131] As far as kindergarten work was concerned, a practice and observation school was established in October, 1893, for the purpose of working with children ages five to eight.[132] Specifically, the Catalogue of 1893-94 stated that the object of the school was "to give the Seniors and those applying for certificates actual practice in methods taught in the pedagogical department."[133] As a part of the requirements, the seniors at the normal school were to work three hours a week in the school and were allowed to observe at other times during the week.[134]

In 1894, Charles D.McIver, President of the Institute, placed an advertisement in the Greensboro Record in an attempt to enroll students from the Greensboro community in the school. The advertisement denoted a shift from emphasizing work with children ages five to eight to work with primary aged children. The advertisement stated:

PRACTICE AND OBSERVATION SCHOOL

The capacity of the model primary school, connected with
The State Normal and Industrial School
having been enlarged, children
will be admitted this year whose
ages are from six to nine years.
There Will Probably Be Three Grades.
This School will begin its work on
            Monday, October 8th.
Tuition Will Be $12.00 a Year.
Application for admission should
be made at once so that the proper
preparations may be made for increased attendance. For further
information apply to
            Charles D. McIver, Pres.[135]

Apparently McIver was not completely satisfied with the normal college placing little emphasis on kindergarten children because in the Report of the Superintendent, 1894-1896, he cited several recommendations for the continued growth of the state school, and among the recommendations was the following:

In addition to the work of the Practice and
Observation School there ought to be a genuine
Kindergarten Department, teaching the most scientific
methods of caring for and training children between
the ages of four and six. I doubt whether the State
could accomplish more good in any other direction with
the same amount of money than by maintaining one model
kindergarten school in connection with the institution
which is to train so many of its teachers and so many

of its women who will not be teachers.[136]

An examination of the reports following the one for 1894-96 revealed no evidence that the recommendation was accepted.

The kindergarten at the Woman's College of the University of North Carolina began operating in September, 1935. Until that time a nursery school associated with the Home Economics Department had been maintained, as had been an elementary school in connection with the Education Department. A link between the nursery school and the elementary school was deemed necessary for the sake of the children enrolled in the laboratory school. Eugenia Hunter was employed as the first teacher in the kindergarten, and she remained in that position for eight years, until she resigned to attend graduate school at Ohio State University. Hunter was succeeded by Mrs. Grace Carter Efird.

From the beginning of the kindergarten at Woman's College, students majoring in primary education observed in the kindergarten and also served as student assistants. Students began completing student teaching requirements for credit in the kindergarten around 1940.

In-service training for teachers in kindergarten work began during the first year the kindergarten was in operation. Invitations were sent to private kindergarten teachers throughout the state once each semester of the school year and approximately twenty-five to thirty people generally accepted. In addition, beginning in 1939, Hunter, who had returned to the Woman's College of the University of North Carolina, began conducting two-week institutes for teachers involved in kindergarten education.

The kindergarten was terminated in 1970, against the protest of many faculty members and parents who had children in the school. The same year, Hunter retired, culminating thirty-five years of work in early childhood education.[137]

Efforts prior to 1940 to establish kindergartens as a part of the public school system of North Carolina had been many and varied. The question "Why shouldn't every town, and every public school in North Carolina, have its kindergarten?" posed by the editor of North Carolina Education in 1923 remained unanswered.[138]

Summary

As early as 1830, newspaper accounts noted that Infant Schools were available for young children in North Carolina. Parents were encouraged to enroll their children in the Infant School as a way of providing a solid foundation for later learning.

During the period prior to 1940, there was both public and private interest in schools for young children in North Carolina. From a legal standpoint, private kindergartens could be maintained by anyone wishing to establish a school, and in 1923, a provision was made by the General Assembly that allowed for the establishment of public kindergartens if the voters of a school district supported the issue.

Much of the interest was expressed by the private sector of the population and only limited opportunities for the training of teachers of young children were available. Beginning in 1878, the University of North Carolina offered courses in kindergarten instruction for approximately fifteen years. Instructors holding the appropriate credentials to teach kindergarten education were brought from New York and Washington, D.D., to offer courses. Four other state-supported teacher-training institutions, Asheville State Normal School, Franklin Normal School, Washington Normal School, and Newton Normal School, offered kindergarten work prior to 1940.

Trinity College in Randolph County, in 1878, and Peace Institute in Raleigh, in 1879, were two private institutions that offered kindergarten instruction and provided a model school in order that teachers might gain practical experience. From 1900 to 1910, another private school, St. Paul's, in Beaufort, provided training for teachers wanting to work with kindergarten children.

Various mills in North Carolina provided kindergartens for the children of their employees. The Bureau of Education reported in 1914 that three mills in the state maintained kindergartens for at least 160 days each year.

Since 1892, the North Carolina Institute for the Deaf and Dumb and the Blind has maintained kindergartens for handicapped children. Recognition was given to the fact that blind children were as much in need of early experiences as were sighted children.

Only two public school systems maintained kindergartens in North Carolina prior to 1940. One system was the Asheville City Schools and the other system was the Washington City Schools. The Asheville kindergartens, initially a gift from the Asheville Free Kindergarten Association, were discontinued in 1930 after the Attorney General rendered the opinion that the kindergartens were illegal because the voters in the district had not passed on the matter.

State and national organizations were interested in the establishment of schools for young children in North Carolina. When E. C. Brooks was Superintendent of Public Instruction, Nina Vandewalker from the United States Bureau of Education, and Bessie Locke from the National Kindergarten Association wrote letters of encouragement to provide kindergartens for the youth of North Carolina.

For several years, the North Carolina Kindergarten Association, a division of the North Carolina Teachers Assembly, met to discuss and exchange ideas about kindergarten work. Guest speakers for several of the meetings included Annie E. George, Ella Victoria Dobbs, and Lucy Gage. In 1920, the North Carolina Congress of Parents and Teachers proposed a resolution in favor of kindergartens as a part of the public school system of North Carolina. The North Carolina Congress has continued its support for public kindergartens since that time.

The State Normal and Industrial School in Greensboro briefly provided a kindergarten in 1893 to assist the normal school students in their work with young children. The following year the observation and participation school placed emphasis on primary children rather than on five-year-old children. In 1935, when the Greensboro institution was known as Woman's College, a kindergarten was established and continued to serve the city and college community until 1970.

Interest in kindergartens had been expressed in North Carolina, but by 1940 no state-wide public-supported program had been established.

CHAPTER III

EFFORTS TO ESTABLISH KINDERGARTENS

FROM 1940-1968

Efforts to establish public kindergartens in North Carolina increased significantly during the period from 1940 to 1968. Several milestones marked the way for legislative action in 1969 that provided money for the establishment of kindergartens as a part of the public school system in North Carolina. The initiation of several federal and foundation programs in North Carolina added to the interest in kindergartens. The programs, in turn, reflected the need for kindergartens as a part of the public school system in order for many children to gain from the educational opportunity of pre-first grade experiences.

From a legal standpoint, during the 1950's, the North Carolina General Assembly restated laws that allowed for kindergartens to be a part of the public school system at the discretion of the voters in each school district. In the 1960's, bills authorizing the establishment of state kindergartens were presented at each session of the legislature, but the actual authority to establish public kindergartens undergirded with funding was not granted until the 1969 legislative session.

Legal Status

In 1945, the General Assembly of North Carolina enacted legislation concerning the education of pre-first grade children. The law, entitled "An Act to Amend the School Machinery Act of One Thousand Nine Hundred and Thirty-Nine, and Other Parts of the School Law," continued to provide for the establishment of public kindergartens in any school district if the voters of that district so desired. In addition, the law stated that kindergarten instruction in any school district, whether public or private, would be under the supervision of the State Department of Public Instruction. Specifically, the section concerning the supervision of kindergartens was expressed as follows:

Such kindergarten instruction as may be established under the provisions of this section, or established in any other manner, shall be subject to the supervision of the State Department of Public Instruction and shall be operated in accordance with standards adopted by the State Board of Education.[1]

In a letter dated March 13, 1971, Patsy Montague, the first supervisor of early childhood education programs to be employed by the State Department of Public Instruction, noted:

> (T)ime and again we had to defend the law which gave
> our _Department_ the right to supervise and evaluate
> nursery schools and kindergartens. This law (Public
> School Law) was, in my opinion, a very vital step in
> the direction of public kindergartens.[2]

In May, 1952, the problem of having "the right to supervise and
evaluate" pre-first grade programs was called to the attention
of the Attorney General of North Carolina by Superintendent
Clyde A. Erwin. Attorney General Harry McMullan ruled that the
law was broad enough to allow the State Department of Public
Instruction to supervise private kindergartens in the State.[3]

In 1955, the General Assembly of North Carolina reaffirmed
its position on the legality of public kindergartens. The legal
status was stated in this manner:

> Such kindergarten schools as may be established
> under the provisions of this section, or established
> in any other manner, shall be subject to the super-
> vision of the State Department of Public Instruction
> and shall be operated in accordance with standards to
> be provided by the State Board of Education.[4]

The 1955 law remained in effect and no new legislation was
introduced to change the law until 1963. At the 1963 legislative session, House Bill 792 was introduced by Representative
Rachel D. Davis from Kinston, and others.

House Bill 792 was significant in that it was the first
time legislation was offered that would establish a state-wide
kindergarten program at public expense. The bill called for
pilot kindergarten programs to be established in selected school
administrative units. The programs in each school unit were to
be considered a part of the regular school program, and the
classes were to serve as laboratories for the training of kindergarten teachers. In addition, the bill provided for a consultant
at the state level to provide assistance and direction to both
private and public kindergartens operating within the state.[5]
The bill failed to pass on second reading on June 3, 1963.[6]

In the legislative session of 1965, Senator Martha Evans,
of Mecklenburg County, and Senator Lennox P. McLendon, Jr., of
Guilford County, introduced Senate Bill 85. The bill provided
for the same measures to establish public kindergartens as did
the 1963 bill, but in shorter form. An appropriation in the
amount of $390,800 for the pilot project was requested for each
year of the biennium. For the kindergartens, $350,000 would have
been appropriated, $20,000 would have gone for scholarships for
teachers to attend institutions offering courses in early childhood education, and $20,800 would have provided consultants at

the State Department of Public Instruction to assist in the development of the kindergartens.[7] The bill was defeated on June 11, 1965.[8]

Evans demonstrated her continued interest in the establishment of public kindergartens when she and two other senators introduced Senate Bill 6 during the 1967 Session of the General Assembly. The 1967 bill was exactly the same as the bill presented in 1965. From the standpoint of appropriations, the bill would have provided $750,000 each year of the biennium to finance the kindergartens, $25,000 in scholarships for one hundred teachers to take courses in early childhood education, and $25,800 for consultants in program development.[9] The last action taken on the bill was on March 23, 1967, when the bill was again referred to the Appropriations Committee.[10]

Legally, at the end of the 1967 Session of the General Assembly, the 1955 law was still in effect. Groundwork had been laid, however, and in the 1969 Session a law was passed that would establish public kindergartens as a part of the public school system of North Carolina.

Probably one of the most significant factors that aided in the establishment of legal provisions for public kindergartens in North Carolina was the Governor's Study Commission. The 1967 General Assembly passed Resolution 81, called "A Joint Resolution Creating a Commission to Study the Public School System of North Carolina." The Resolution granted authority to Governor Dan K. Moore and to others to appoint certain North Carolinians to serve on the Commission to study the public school system in the state. The findings of the study were to be presented to the Governor by October 1, 1968, and he, in turn, was to present the findings to the 1969 General Assembly.[11]

Upon completion of the study, top priority was given to establishing kindergartens as a part of the public school system in North Carolina. More details on the recommendations made by the Commission concerning public kindergartens will be presented in Chapter IV.

Efforts of the State Department of Public Instruction

The literature reveiwed indicated that interest in kindergartens and efforts to establish kindergartens as a part of the public school system in North Carolina were in evidence during the decade of the 1940's. There is a letter to Clyde Erwin from Anne Rabe, Supervising Teacher, First Grade, Western Carolina Teachers College, that indicated such interest. The letter was written in response to Erwin's suggestion that the number of years in public school be extended upward to twelve years. As an alternative to the plan, Rabe suggested that a pre-primary or a "Junior Primary" section be set up as a downward extension of the public school program. The pre-primary plan would aid the children in the transition from home to school.[12] Rabe's

suggestion was not accepted; but in 1951, ten years after
Rabe's letter to Erwin, Patsy Montague, a person with credentials
in early childhood education, was added to the staff of the State
Department of Public Instruction, indicating an interest in pre-
primary education in the state.

Greater importance was given early childhood education in
the 1950's. Patsy Montague was the first person with a degree
in early childhood education to be employed by the State Department
of Public Instruction. Erwin, State Superintendent of Public
Instruction from 1934-1952, talked with Montague in 1951 and
indicated to her that he desired to employ a person with an early
childhood education degree and experience in kindergarten work.
Montague joined the State Department of Public Instruction shortly
after the interview with Erwin. Montague's title was Elementary
Supervisor, and she was asked to assist in the writing of the
first bulletin on standards for public and private kindergartens
in the state.[13]

Shortly after Montague joined the staff of elementary supervisors at the State Department, J. Everette Miller, Assistant
Superintendent of Public Instruction, at the request of Erwin,
set up a series of meetings to aid the supervisors in formulating
plans to write the bulletin of standards. The following year,
1952, Erwin died; work on the bulletin was delayed. Charles F.
Carroll succeeded Erwin as State Superintendent of Public Instruction and work on the bulletin was resumed.[14] The bulletin of
standards for kindergartens in North Carolina was entitled Schools
for Young Children and was published by the State Department
of Public Instruction in 1955 after several years of preparation.

In 1961, a supervisor for non-public schools was added to
the staff of the State Department of Public Instruction. In 1968,
the Division of Early Childhood Education was organized and was
assigned the responsibility of implementing the pilot kindergarten program in North Carolina. The same year, a supervisor
for non-public kindergartens was employed.

The duties of the non-public kindergarten supervisor consist
mainly of assisting private kindergartens in their efforts to
gain approval of the State Department of Public Instruction. A
three-page check list is sent to each kindergarten requesting
state approval, and the supervisor reviews the report and recommends what action should be taken. The supervisor is concerned
with teacher certification, the type of program offered, and the
physical facilities of the school. In order to receive state
approval, the director of a non-public kindergarten must hold
a K-3 certificate and have a minimum of two years of teaching
experience.[15]

Since 1950, the Biennial Report of the Superintendent of
Public Instruction has contained recommendations that encouraged
kindergartens as an educational opportunity for the pre-first
grade children in North Carolina. In the 1950-52 Report, Superintendent Clyde A. Erwin recommended "broadening the scope of
our public school system to include kindergarten education."[16]

The same Report noted that private kindergartens in the state were growing in numbers, and that the growth indicated public interest in early childhood education in North Carolina.[17]

The Report for 1952-54 encouraged public support of kindergartens. In it, Superintendent Charles F. Carroll stated:

> A tax-supported program of public kindergarten education in some communities in North Carolina, with well-qualified teachers and an appropriate instructional program, and conducted in accordance with State standards of operation, appears imperative as our people continue to express their belief in the worth of education at levels below and beyond the scope of our present twelve-year system.[18]

In the 1954-56 Report and in the 1956-58 Report, Carroll recommended that supervisors in early childhood education be added to the personnel of the State Department of Public Instruction.[19]

Signs of strong interest to establish kindergartens as a part of the public school system in North Carolina appeared in the decade of the 1960's. The 1960-62 Report recommended that kindergarten education be made available to all children in the state.[20] In the 1962-64 Report, Carroll noted the growth of private kindergartens in the state, and in the 1964-66 Report expressed his view that North Carolina should extend the scope of public education by adding kindergartens to the public school system.[21]

In the 1966-68 Report, Carroll again recommended kindergartens as a part of the public school system and, in so doing, offered stronger and more supportive data than had been presented in prior reports. In a section of the 1966-68 Report entitled "Looking to the Future," he made the following statement:

> Kindergarten and Early Childhood Education should be initiated on a nine months' optional basis. In support of this extension of the public school system it is generally acknowledged that organized pre-school experiences in education greatly enhance the probability of success in school. Preferably before children attain the age of four, their physical, mental, psychological, and emotional deficiencies should be identified and corrected. These corrections, which would greatly accelerate learning, should be provided at State expense for indigent children.[22]

The year 1968 was to become an eventful one and a turning point in establishing kindergartens as a part of the public school system in North Carolina. The Governor's Commission to study the public school system of the state would offer significant recommendations concerning kindergartens.

East Carolina Teachers College first provided kindergarten and nursery school education through course work offered through the Department of Home Economics at the institution. The first such course was listed in the Catalogue of East Carolina Teachers College, 1944-45, and was entitled "Kindergarten and Nursery School Seminar."[23] For the academic years 1945-46 and 1946-47 the same course continued to be listed in the Catalogue, but no such course was listed in the Catalogue for the academic year 1947-48.[24]

East Carolina Teachers College then opened a kindergarten in September, 1948. John D. Messick, President of the College, and Dora Coates, a member of the Department of Education, proposed that the kindergarten should "stimulate interest in schools for 5-year-old children in line with the emphasis of that time, and to serve as a valuable supplement to the teacher-training program for the Primary field."[25]

Annie Mae Murray was the person chosen to be the teacher in the kindergarten, a position she held until 1966. In conjunction with the kindergarten, a course called "Observation and Participation in the Kindergarten" was established. Students observed in the kindergarten and were directly involved with the children in the program. To add "an understanding of the philosophy, curriculum, etc. of kindergarten education" the students and Murray met weekly to discuss problems and situations in which the students had been involved. According to Murray, most of the students enjoyed their work with the children and many expressed an interest in teaching in kindergartens.[26]

Except for the North Carolina School for the Blind, East Carolina Teachers College and Woman's College in Greensboro were the only state-supported kindergartens in the 1940's and many teachers from around the state went to the institutions to observe kindergarten education. Because of the interest shown, Murray conducted a survey designed to assess the desire for workshops and courses in kindergarten education. The results of Murray's survey indicated that a number of teachers would like additional study in kindergarten teaching; and in 1952, Murray conducted her first workshop for teachers. During the 1953 workshop, the North Carolina Kindergarten Association, an organization mainly composed of people associated with private kindergartens in the state, was established.[27]

Interest Expressed by School-Related Organizations

After 1940, the North Carolina Congress of Parents and Teachers continued to express interest in the establishment of kindergartens as a part of the public school system in the state. During the 1950's and 1960's, the North Carolina Education Associ-

ation and the North Carolina Teachers Association began to express
some interest in schools for five-year-old children in North
Carolina.

North Carolina Congress of Parents and Teachers. In 1920,
the North Carolina Congress of Parents and Teachers first expressed
interest in the downward extension of the state public school
system to include kindergartens. The interest of the North
Carolina Congress in public kindergartens continued to grow as
the organization grew.

Since 1945 the department of the Congress designed to function in the interest of young children has been called Pre-School
Service. The section mainly provided study groups for parents
whose children would soon enter first grade and emphasized health
programs through cooperative work in local communities.[28]

During the decade of the 1960's, the legislative program
of the North Carolina Congress emphasized more than ever before
the need for public kindergartens in North Carolina. As part
of the program for 1961-63, the North Carolina Congress endorsed
kindergartens by stating that "to secure for every child the
highest advantages of physical, mental, social, and spiritual
education, we shall work for. . .emphasis on pre-school education. . ."[29] As part of the platform for 1963-66, the North
Carolina Congress continued to support public kindergartens in
North Carolina. As stated by the Congress, one of the purposes
stated in the platform was: "Realizing that in order to secure
for every child all that he is capable of becoming, we shall
move forward with new understanding:. . .of the need to extend
educational opportunity from pre-school through education beyond
high school."[30] Further, the North Carolina Congress called
for the financial support of kindergartens as part of the public
school system of the state. The 1968 Convention strongly advocated public kindergartens and made its position known by
passing the following resolution:

> Whereas, since 1920 the North Carolina Congress
> of Parents and Teachers has endorsed the idea of
> state-supported kindergartens; and
> Whereas, a number of previous studies have indicated
> a need for such a program; and
> Whereas, the Special Committee to Study Public
> Schools has been directed to determine the feasibility
> of such a program; and
> Whereas, the 1967 Convention passed a resolution
> of full support, be it therefore,
> Resolved that the North Carolina Congress of
> Parents and Teachers urges the next General Assembly to
> establish a full kindergarten program in North Carolina.[31]

North Carolina Education Association and the North Carolina Teachers Association. Since 1956 the North Carolina Educa-

tion Association has offered some support to public kindergartens. The legislative program of the organization has mainly advocated a reduction in class size and an increase in teachers' salaries; however, support for state kindergartens was expressed under the heading "Other pressing needs." According to Glenn Keever, editor of North Carolina Education, the North Carolina Education Association chose to support the appropriation of state funds for the benefit of teachers rather than for new educational programs, since funds were limited.[32]

In 1964, the North Carolina Education Association asked 18,000 members to rank their preferences as to what they wanted the organization to support during the up-coming session of the General Assembly. Seventh in the list following the reduction of class size, increased salaries, special teachers, tenure, clerical aid for teachers, and teachers for retarded and talented children, was state-supported kindergartens.[33]

Another survey to determine the interests of the membership of the North Carolina Education Association was conducted in 1968. The membership ranked public kindergartens higher than in 1964. The kindergartens then had reached the fifth spot of priorities set by the membership, following salary increases, reduction of class and teacher load, special teachers, and teacher and clerical aids.[34] Again, as indicated by the survey, the interests of the members of the North Carolina Education Association seemed to be in favor of teacher benefits rather than new education programs in the state.

Some people reason that since the North Carolina Education Association represented the educators in the state, the organization supported the areas of major concern to mainly teachers. Public kindergartens were supported by the association, but largely as a secondary concern.

The North Carolina Teachers Association adopted a resolution to support public kindergartens in April, 1963, at the 82nd Annual Convention of the organization. The resolution stated:

> Whereas, there are differences in the maturity, economic, social and cultural background of beginning children, and
> Whereas, it is believed that systematic training and guidance for the pre-school child is essential for future growth and development.
> BE IT RESOLVED: That we urge the establishment of publicly supported kindergartens in the North Carolina Public Schools.[35]

The resolution continued to be reaffirmed at each convention of the North Carolina Teachers Association until 1969.[36] In 1970, the North Carolina Teachers Association and the North Carolina Education Association merged into one professional organization, and the new association, the North Carolina Association of

Educators, continued to maintain support of public kindergartens.

A personal interview with E. B. Palmer and telephone conversations with Ruth L. Woodson and Alfonso Elder did not reveal any additional information concerning the efforts of the black community in North Carolina to establish public kindergartens, although private kindergartens for black children have been in operation in the state for many years.[37]

Kindergartens in the Public Schools in the State

Information was available concerning two kindergartens in the state during the 1960's that were housed and partially financed by public funds. One of the programs, located in Orange County, was conducted as a part of the study of rural children in North Carolina. The other kindergarten program was established and financed by the Roanoke Rapids school system. The Orange County and Roanoke Rapids programs were the first kindergartens supported by funds earmarked for public schools since the kindergartens were established in Asheville and Washington.

Orange County Kindergarten Program, 1963-65. Dr. Emmett Baughman, a psychologist at the University of North Carolina, conducted a child study project at the Efland and Efland-Cheeks schools in Orange County during the years 1963 to 1965. Since money was available to employ teachers, Dr. Baughman requested that a kindergarten program be initiated in the two schools as a part of the project.

After Baughman's request for a kindergarten program in the two schools, G. P. Carr, Superintendent of Orange County Schools, wrote a letter to Charles F. Carroll, State Superintendent of Public Instruction, and requested clarification of the legality of the proposed kindergarten program in terms of age, transportation, and the lunchroom program.[38]

Carroll referred Carr's letter to the Office of the Attorney General. In a letter dated February 23, 1962, Ralph Moody, Assistant Attorney General, responded to Carr's questions. Moody stated that since North Carolina had permissive legislation concerning kindergartens, the two schools in Orange County would be within legal authority to enroll children younger than six years of age. Moody noted also that since federal funds were to be used to operate the program, no problems concerning state budgetary matters would be involved.[39] The kindergartens operated from 1963 to 1965.

Roanoke Rapids Public Kindergartens. In 1964, the Board of Education in the Roanoke Rapids Graded School District considered the feasibility of a kindergarten program for the school district. After three years of discussion and study, the Board appointed a six-member committee to investigate further the possibilities of a kindergarten program for Roanoke Rapids schools.

After studying the literature on kindergarten programs

from various part of the United States, the six-member committee recommended that the Board of Education provide for a kindergarten program in the Roanoke Rapids schools beginning in September, 1968. The program was made available to every five-year-old child in the district, and 95 percent of the children responded by enrolling in the schools. According to Superintendent Talley, the teachers and facilities have been upgraded each year since the beginning of the program and efforts have continued in the Roanoke Rapids Graded School District to develop a suitable instructional program for the five-year-olds in the district.[40]

Federal and Foundation Programs for Young Children

Several federal and foundation programs have allocated funds to North Carolina to be used to provide pre-first grade experiences for children. As far as the federal programs are concerned, Project Head Start and Title I of the Elementary and Secondary Education Act have probably made the greatest impact on the education of five-year-old children in North Carolina. The Ford Foundation, in cooperation with the State Board of Education, provided funds for the Comprehensive School Improvement Project, part of which was a summer program for young children.

The Comprehensive School Improvement Project. The Comprehensive School Improvement Project began in the summer of 1964 with the Summer Readiness Program. The project was funded by the State Board of Education and the Ford Foundation, and was administered by the State Department of Public Instruction. One of the main purposes of the Summer Readiness Program of the Project was as follows: "To improve the preparation of selected preschool youth for successful entry into the first grade of the public schools of the State."[41]

The Project was designed to operate in a public school under the supervision of persons in the local school district. The proposed thrust of the program was toward the improvement of reading, writing, and arithmetic in the primary grades in terms of both the teaching and the learning process; and one special aspect was for kindergarten children.[42] The children came to school for four hours a day, five days a week, for a period of thirty days. Priority in selection of the children to attend the program was given to the culturally disadvantaged.

Activities and material used for instructional purposes were developed through memebers of the CSIP staff in cooperation with members of the State Department of Public Instruction, and consultants from various colleges and universities in the state offered assistance. The materials and activities were designed to provide appropriate experiences for the culturally disadvantaged children who would be served by the program in the hope that school success would be enhanced.[43]

Evaluation of the Summer Readiness Program indicated that

teachers and principals involved came to know and understand the children better than they had before. Ninety-five percent of the principals and teachers stated that they felt that better provisions were made for individual differences because of the flexible school day.[44]

The Summer Readiness Program of the Comprehensive School Improvement Project continued to function until 1967. Because of several federal programs in operation in North Carolina, the readiness program terminated its work but had left its influence by demonstrating the worth of educational programs for young children.

Project Head Start. The Economic Opportunity Act of 1964 included Project Head Start, a program designed to meet the educational needs of young children from poverty families.[45] The pilot Head Start program, launched in 1965 with an initial appropriation of $96.4 million, was an eight-weeks summer program for children who would enter first grade in the fall.[46] The State Board of Education in North Carolina entered into the agreement to participate in Head Start programs on April 1, 1965.[47]

The national objectives of Project Head Start were directed basically toward strengthening a child's sense of dignity and self-worth. Specifically, the objectives were as follows:

1. Meeting physical, nutrition, and dental needs.
2. Strengthening emotional and social development by encouraging self-confidence, spontaneity, curiosity, and self-discipline.
3. Stimulating mental processes and skills, with particular attention to conceptual and verbal aspects.
4. Establishing and reinforcing patterns and expectations of success to promote self-confidence.
5. Increasing the child's capacity to relate positively to family and community, while at the same time strengthening the family's capacity to contribute to the child's development.
6. Fostering in the child and his family a responsible attitude toward society, while stimulating constructive opportunities for the poor to work together on a personal and community basis toward the solution of their problems.[48]

Project Head Start was designed in such a way that the programs were developed and administered at the local level under the auspices of regional coordinators. Jenny W. Klein, Senior Educational Specialist, Project Head Start, stated: "The most appropriate local programs are determined by a group of parents and community representatives working in a policy committee."[49]

Project Head Start remained under the Office of Economic Opportunity until July 1, 1969, when the authority for the project was delegated to the Office of Child Development, U. S. Department of Health, Education, and Welfare. Since local control was to be at the core of the Head Start Programs, each individual locality in North Carolina providing such a program would be somewhat different, in accordance with the needs of each community. Suffice it to say that Project Head Start played a part in demonstrating to the people of North Carolina that pre-first grade programs could make a contribution to the education of young children.

Elementary and Secondary Education Act, Title I. In 1965, the State Board of Education entered into an agreement with the U. S. Office of Education to administer Title I, ESEA of 1965. The result of the agreement was that the State of North Carolina could receive federal funds under Public Law 89-10.[50] Actual operation of Title I in North Carolina began in the spring of 1966.

Title I funds are to be used only for children who can be catagorized as educationally deprived. The following criteria have been set up as guidelines to assist in identifying educationally deprived children:

1. Children with composite scores below the 25th percentile on standardized achievement test batteries.
2. Children who have been retained a year or more in school.
3. Children who have intelligence quotient scores of 89 or below or who score below the 25th percentile on intelligence tests or tests of scholastic aptitude.
4. Children who score one grade level or more below their actual grade placement on composite scores of achievement test batteries.
5. Children who perform lower than expected according to their age on readiness tests or inventories of readiness.
6. Children of school age who have dropped out of school prior to graduation from high school.
7. Children who present evidence of maladjusted social behavior which may interfere with their success in school.
8. Children who are handicapped; this includes emotionally, mentally, or physically handicapped children.
9. Children who have very unsatisfactory attendance records.
10. Children who have behavioral problems which seriously interfere with their learning.
11. Children who present evidence of future unsatisfactory school adjustment because of environmental background. This may include the children of migratory agricultural workers and minority, social or ethnic groups.[51]

During the school year 1967-68, approximately 16,000 children participated in Title I kindergarten projects in North Carolina.[52] By 1969, sixty-three local school units were providing either a summer readiness program or a full-year kindergarten program through Title I funds. Approximately 12,000 children participated in the programs for the year 1968-69. For the school year 1970-71, sixty-six school units provided kindergartens through Title I funds and served approximately 10,000 five-year-olds in North Carolina.[53]

Summary

From 1940 to 1968 efforts to establish public kindergartens in North Carolina significantly increased. From a legal standpoint, the General Assembly reiterated the provision that any district in North Carolina could establish kindergartens at the will of the voters, and a new section was added that required the State Department of Public Instruction to supervise all kindergartens in the state. Although three bills were introduced in the General Assembly in the 1960's that would establish kindergartens as a part of the public school system of North Carolina, none was accepted by the legislative body.

In 1948, East Carolina Teachers College began operating a kindergarten in connection with the Department of Education. The kindergarten was to be a supplement to the teacher-training program at the College. In addition to working with children in the kindergarten, the students were offered courses specifically designed to provide information about the young child.

The North Carolina Congress of Parents and Teachers continued its interest and support of schools for five-year-old children. Pre-school services were provided to assist parents of children who would soon enter first grade, and the legislative programs of the North Carolina Congress re-emphasized the importance of public kindergartens for the children of the state. The North Carolina Education Association first offered some support for public kindergartens in 1956, and since becoming the North Carolina Association of Educators has increasingly recognized the need to provide pre-first grade experiences for children.

Two school districts in North Carolina took advantage of the opportunity to provide kindergartens for their children. In the early 1960's, two Orange County schools maintained kindergartens as a part of a program to study a section of the rural South. In 1968, the Roanoke Rapids Graded School District opened kindergartens for all five-year-olds in the district, and 95 percent of the children in the district enrolled. The kindergartens in the Orange County and Roanoke Rapids districts were the first kindergartens to be a part of the public school system since the Asheville kindergartens closed in 1930.

Federal programs added a dimension to the interest in kindergartens in North Carolina. Programs under the Elementary and Secondary Education Act, Title I, assisted many children in the state to become better acquainted with school experience and the kinds of situations encountered there. Project Head Start began in North Carolina in 1965 and provided many experiences to enable children to acquire the needed skills as they prepared to enter kindergarten or first grade.

Private and public funds were pooled in an effort to assist pre-first grade children in meeting the first grade experiences. The Comprehensive School Improvement Project, funded by the State Board of Education and the Ford Foundation, provided educational opportunities for children identified as potential first grade failures in terms of school success. The Summer Readiness Program of the Project was terminated in 1967, but most of the teachers and principals who had been involved in the program felt that the Project had functioned well in its attempt to aid in the educational future of many of the children of North Carolina.

By 1968, much emphasis had been placed on the education of young children. One result was that many interested people in North Carolina began to see the way clear for establishing kindergartens as an integral part of the public school system.

CHAPTER IV

EXTENSION OF THE PUBLIC SCHOOL SYSTEM

TO INCLUDE KINDERGARTEN

The Governor's Study Commission on the Public School System of North Carolina gave priority to establishing a state kindergarten program. The emphasis placed on early childhood education programs in the Commission's report served to provide the necessary impetus to encourage the legislative session of 1969 to propose and enact legislation which authorized the State Board of Education to initiate kindergarten programs in the public schools.

After enactment of the necessary legislation by the General Assembly in 1969, the State Department of Public Instruction made its first attempts to bring into reality a state-wide kindergarten program. An opening ceremony was held in December, 1969, and on that date a kindergarten program duly authorized by the legislature officially began in the public school system of North Carolina.

Governor's Study Commission

Some have suggested that one of the most important factors that influenced the establishment of state kindergartens was the Governor's Study Commission. The Honorable Dan K. Moore, Governor of North Carolina from 1964-68, made a recommendation to the General Assembly in 1967 urging the creation of a Commission to study the public school system in North Carolina. The Commission was set up, and over five hundred North Carolinians participated in the study. The data gathered in the study, as well as recommendations of the Commission, were presented for consideration to the 1969 General Assembly.

Interest in early childhood education seemed to be at an all-time high in North Carolina. More position papers were written for the Commission about kindergartens than about any other area of study except human values.[1] As a result, top priority was given to the establishment of kindergartens in North Carolina, along with occupational education.[2] According to the Commission, such a program for five-year-olds in the state would be one way to enhance human values. The Commission stated in Recommendation 21:

> The establishment of a statewide public kindergarten system should be given top priority. The early years are the crucial years in the development of the concepts of self-respect and responsibility. Public kindergartens are mentioned here because of their potential for developing values.[3]

A survey of classroom teachers conducted by the Commission in March, 1968, provided information concerning the position of classroom teachers on issues that were being studied by the Governor's Study Commission. The survey included a random sample of classroom teachers in the state, and of the 1200 questionnaires distributed, 788 were returned. Item 11 dealt with the subject of kindergartens, and the question was posed as follows:

The Governor's Study Commission is directed to study early childhood education including the feasibility of establishing public kindergartens in the State. What is your opinion?
- a. I believe we should now establish public kindergartens.
- b. I believe we should concentrate first on improving the quality of education in grades 1-12 before considering kindergartens.
- c. I believe that the establishment of kindergartens should be a local, not a State, responsibility.
- d. I do not believe that we in public elementary/ secondary education should be concerned with public kindergartens.[4]

Of the 788 respondents, 64 percent expressed the belief that kindergartens should be established, 30 percent indicated that more emphasis should be placed on improving grades 1-12, 3 percent expressed the belief that the establishment of kindergartens was a local matter, and 3 percent indicated that public education should not be concerned with kindergartens.[5]

As a part of the Commission study, several recommendations pertained especially to a state kindergarten program. Recommendations 36, 37, and 38 strongly supported a state kindergarten program. Recommendation 36 stated: "The Commission recommends that the State of North Carolina extend public education to five-year-olds on the same basis that educational programs are established for other age levels (grades 1-12) as soon as possible."[6] To implement the recommendation, certain amendments to existing laws were necessary. The 1969 General Assembly enacted legislation which provided for an educational program for five-year-olds in the state. Section 6 of the Act stated that "all laws and clauses of laws in conflict with this Act are hereby repealed."[7]

Recommendation 37 dealt with the gradual growth of the kindergarten program. The recommendation stated: "The Commission recommends that the State Board of Education set the necessary policies for a two or three phase effort in establishing public kindergartens, with the initial effort being for 25 percent of the eligible children."[8] A survey of the school superintendents conducted by the Commission indicated that the major problems in setting up a state-wide kindergarten program were staffing and providing adequate housing facilities for the program. In the survey, the superintendents were asked if their administrative unit could plan for kindergartens by the 1969-70 school year. A few of the superintendents stated that they could plan for all eligible children in the district. Ninety-one of the 136 superintendents responded that they could plan for 28,980 children, which was more than one-fourth of the population to be served.[9] When the Kindergarten-Early Childhood Education Division of the State Department of Public Instruction implemented the plans for a kindergarten program, they adhered to Recommendation 37, and 25 percent of the eligible children in the state were enrolled in state-supported kindergartens.

Recommendation 38 was concerned with a continuous progress approach to the organizational pattern of the kindergarten program. Specifically, the recommendation was:

> The Commission recommends that the State Board of Education set policies which initiate for children, ages five through eight, a program of continuous learning that is based upon the individual child's need, interest, and stages of development; and that this program approach the non-graded structure of organization to the extent that particular pupils, personnel, and school resources allow.[10]

The kindergarten, according to the Commission, should be an integral part of the public elementary school and should be planned with enough flexibility to provide successful learning experiences for the children entering the program. The Commission suggested that the class size should be approximately 18-20 students, and that these students should remain at school for three to three and one-half hours per day. An additional suggestion was that the classroom personnel should include a teacher and an aide or an assistant, with some provision for released time for teachers so that they might plan work and engage in conferences with parents.[11] The Kindergarten-Early Childhood Education Division of the State Department of Public Instruction followed the recommendation when the public kindergarten program was implemented in 1969.

Since priority was given to the offering of a kindergarten program in the state, the Commission recommended that the state establish certification requirments for teachers in the area of early childhood education. Concerning the early childhood education certificate, the Commission stated that "this certificate would indicate that the holder is qualified to teach in the grades kindergarten through 3."[12] Specific courses for the preparation of teachers to be certified in early childhood education were not designated by the Commission, but areas of proficiency were mentioned. The Commission suggested:

Training for this certificate should emphasize growth and development during the childhood years from five through eight. The teacher should have training in art and music, plus more general education in academic areas. In teaching, emphasis should be placed on the ability to teach communication skills, especially reading.[13]

The Division of Teacher Education of the State Department of Public Instruction acted upon the recommendation of the Commission as was reflected by the bulletin of certification practices and policies, entitled Teaching in North Carolina, in 1969. Prior to the establishment of kindergartens as a part of the public school system, the certificate held by teachers in grades 1 through 3 was called Primary Certificate.[14] With the introduction into the state of public kindergartens, the certificate was changed to Early Childhood Education Certificate. The main difference in the two certificates was that of suggesting that the state-approved institutions offering work in early childhood education gear the courses to include information about the younger child.

Legal Status

Permissive legislation had been granted to establish public kindergartens in 1923. The law provided any school district with authority to support a public kindergarten if the voters of the district so desired. Proposals to establish kindergartens on a state-wide basis were introduced during every legislative session of the 1960s. All proposals were defeated prior to the bill presented to the 1969 General Assembly.

Senate Bill 109, entitled "An Act to Authorize the State Board of Education to Establish Kindergarten Programs for Five-Year-Olds," was sponsored by Senator Martha Evans and twelve other senators. The bill, introduced on February 19, 1969, called for the establishment of kindergartens as a part of the public school system of North Carolina. The bill also provided for the establishment of programs in early childhood education in the various teacher education institutions in the state, for in-service instruction of teachers, and for guidance services from the State Department of Public Instruction to assist in the program development.[15] The bill allowed children to attend school if their fifth birthday came before October 15 of the year in which they were to be enrolled in school.

When Senator Evans first introduced the bill, $18 million was asked as the appropriation. The bill passed July 1, 1969, with an appropriation of $1 million.[16] Lack of sufficient funds to finance several educational needs in the state was one of the reasons given for the drastic reduction. The 1969-71 budget contained no recommendations for the funding of a kindergarten program, but in his budget message to the 1969 General Assembly,

Robert W. Scott, Governor of North Carolina, requested $1 million for a pilot kindergarten program. In a letter dated June 2, 1972, Scott stated:

> In 1969, there were not enough General Fund resources to fund all of the new programs and salary increases I endorsed; and there was such fierce competition for appropriations (including requests from the teachers to raise salaries to the national average) that it was necessary for me to recommend General Fund tax increases to provide some $95 million of additional resources. Most of these funds were required to give the teachers a 10 percent salary increase in 1969-70 and an additional 10 percent increase for 1970-71, and there was only enough left to fund a very limited kindergarten program.[17]

Organization and Administration of the Kindergarten Program

After the 1969 bill granting the State Board of Education the legal authority to establish public kindergartens, plans were made to place one early childhood demonstration center in each of the eight educational districts. In order to implement the plan, State Superintendent of Public Instruction A. Craig Phillips invited 153 school districts in North Carolina to submit proposals to obtain a demonstration center, and seventy school districts applied.[18]

At the July 3, 1969, meeting of the State Board of Education guidelines were approved for establishing the eight demonstration centers which would begin public kindergartens in North Carolina. The guidelines outlined the primary functions of the centers as being:

(1) develop and implement kindergarten programs as an integral part of effective educational programs for young children, ages 5-8
(2) develop, in cooperation with higher education institutions, effective training programs for professional and para-professional personnel
(3) directly involve parents in the development and implementation of such programs
(4) develop ways and means of inter-agency (regional agencies, health and welfare) collaboration and cooperation in serving the needs of young children
(5) develop comprehensive and effective programs of evaluation for each aspect of the program
(6) provide information about the program for dissemination throughout the State.[19]

49

Although seventy school systems had submitted proposals to obtain an early childhood demonstration center, only eight school systems could be selected. The State Board of Education set up criteria for selecting the schools that would participate in the kindergarten program. The Board requested that the Division of Kindergarten-Early Childhood Education of the State Department of Public Instruction take the following into consideration:

1. A committment of the school board, school administration, and the school staff to develop and operate a unique and creative program, based on the needs of young children, in a Demonstration Center.
   A. Recognition of the fact that the Center located in their community is a part of a state-wide network of such Centers.
   B. A willingness to work cooperatively with personnel from outside the school system, including personnel from the Department of Public Instruction, the Learning Institute of North Carolina and institutions of higher education, in program development, implementation, and evaluation.
   C. The identification and training (pre-service and in-service) professional and para-professional personnel in cooperation with teacher-training institutions, high schools, community colleges, and other institutions and agencies.
2. Personnel Considerations
   A. A school principal who is willing and able to direct the various functions of the Demonstration Centers.
   B. A teaching staff that meets the following qualifications:
      1. Have training and/or experience in early childhood education.
      2. Are prepared to plan with other teachers (individuals and groups) to implement the various functions of training, parent involvement, evaluation, and dissemination of information.
      3. Are willing to work in a non-graded, continuous progress school program.
   C. The provision of a staff that is balanced ethnically (administrators, teachers, and service personnel)
   D. The provision of special service personnel (food, transportation, art, music, health, etc.,) as needed, to the program of the Demonstration Centers.
3. Facility Considerations
   A. A school building with space for 40 to 120 five-year-old children. This might be a separate

primary unit, or it might be a part of an elementary school.

    B. Involvement of the Division of School Planning in renovating and furnishing kindergarten rooms.

    C. Provision of observational facilities large enough to serve reasonable pre-service and in-service training functions.

    D. Appropriate space for adult conferences and classes.

    E. Adequate and well-equipped outdoor areas.

4. School Population Considerations

    A. Stable (non-transient) community population in order to insure that a high percentage of children entering kindergarten will remain for at least four years.

    B. Pupil enrollment that represents a true socio-economic cross section of the administrative unit. (Some of the Centers will be located in rural areas some in small towns, and some in urban areas.)[20]

On August 7, 1969, the Board of Education approved the eight project proposals and the following schools were selected:

1. Chocowinity Primary School
    Chocowinity, North Carolina
2. Beaufort Elementary School
    Beaufort, North Carolina
3. Jeffreys Grove School
    Raleigh, North Carolina
4. Southern Pines Elementary School
    Southern Pines, North Carolina
5. Saxapahaw Elementary School
    Graham, North Carolina
6. Woodhill Elementary School
    Gastonia, North Carolina
7. East Harper Elementary School
    Lenoir, North Carolina
8. Sylva Elementary School
    Sylva, North Carolina[21]

The objectives of the kindergarten program were formulated by members of the staff at the State Department of Public Instruction, selected superintendents, pricipals and teachers, and consultants from the Appalachian Regional Commission, an organization established during the administration of John F. Kennedy for the purpose of assisting Appalachian counties from Massachusetts to Georgia. The objectives were designed to center around the children that the program was to serve. Specifically, the program objectives were:

    (a) To provide many opportunities for social development and adjustment to group living.

(b) To promote development of good health habits.

(c) To instill habits, appreciations, and attitudes which serve as standards of conduct at work and play and as guides to worthwhile use of time and materials in and out of school.

(d) To provide opportunity for self-expression through language, music, art, and self-experiences.

(e) To provide situations in which the child can succeed and, through success, build confidence in his own ability and work.

(f) To develop an atmosphere in which creativity is stimulated.

(g) To develop a feeling of adequacy through emphasis on independence and good work habits.

(h) To lay foundations for subject matter learning and intellectual growth.[22]

After the early childhood demonstration centers had been designated and program objectives had been formulated, the next step was to provide training and supervision for the personnel involved in the centers. The Learning Institute of North Carolina sponsored a one-month summer institute for the purpose of acquainting those persons in the administration of the eight centers with quality programs in early childhood education.[23] The training session was held in July, 1969, at the Eliot-Pearson Child Study Center at Tufts University, in Medford, Massachusetts.

The program at Tufts University was chosen as a place to visit and study because it utilized some of the components of the British Infant School. The components emphasized the "child's basic characteristics, activeness, and inquisitiveness," and North Carolina was considering the adoption of these components for the kindergarten program.[24]

Thirty-six persons attended, including one person from each of twenty school systems in the state, four university professors, three staff members of the State Department of Public Instruction, and several members of the staff of the Learning Institute of North Carolina. Those persons attending the sessions at Tufts were chosen because of their leadership potential as key people in education.

Activities of the institute included observations of the early childhood education programs in the Eliot-Pearson Children's School and the Boston area, and lectures and films presented by the staff at Eliot-Pearson. In addition, lecturers such as Professor Emeritus Abigail Eliot, founder of the Eliot-Pearson Child Study Center, and Dr. Burton White, Director of the Preschool Project, Harvard University, offered their expertise.[25]

On December 1, 1969, the eight demonstration centers opened. At Jeffreys Grove School, in Wake County, Governor Robert W. Scott and State Superintendent of Public Instruction A. Craig Phillips officially opened the kindergartens. All eight centers were able to participate in the ceremony via telephone.[26]

The enrollment for the first year was 320 children. The average age of the children entering school was five years six months.[27] For the purpose of evaluation and to insure a representation of each district, the children who attended the early childhood demonstration centers were selected on the basis of a stratified sample regarding race, age, sex, and socio-economic status.[28]

The centers altered the concept of the conventional classroom by placing the focus on interest centers which encouraged the children to make choices as to what they desired to be involved with in a learning situation. Two teachers and two assistants were employed for every forty children.[29] The teacher's role was to be one of "guide, counselor, resource person, and director of learning activities rather than a dispenser of knowledge."[30]

Each center had observation booths as well as facilities for conferences with visitors who wished to discuss the program. Parents were encouraged to visit the classroom, and many frequently took the opportunity to observe their chidren in the program.[31]

Training for the personnel involved in the North Carolina kindergarten program continued in the summer of 1970. Two institutes were held during the time, one in the western section of North Carolina and one in the eastern section.

One institute was held at East Carolina University and was sponsored by the State Department of Public Instruction, the Learning Institute of North Carolina, and the Beaufort County schools. The institute to serve the western part of the state was held at the University of North Carolina at Charlotte, and was sponsored by the State Department of Public Instruction, the Learning Institute of North Carolina, and the Gaston County schools.[32]

The institutes were planned for administrators and teachers who would be involved in working in the centers during the 1970-71 school year. Major emphasis was placed upon working with multi-aged continuous progress programs. As a part of the experiences provided, the participants were given the opportunity of working with children in a special summer enrichment program. Open education based on some of the practices of the British Infant Schools was planned.[33] The program was child-centered, and utilized "an active, manipulative curriculum" which gave "children a chance to make choices and teachers a chance to guide interests into all kinds of concept, development, skills, etc. (sic)."[34]

At the February 5, 1970, meeting of the State Board of Education, funds were allocated to open ten additional centers for the 1970-71 academic year. The State Superintendent of Public Instruction was instructed to invite local boards of education to submit a letter which expressed the desire to obtain a kindergarten-early childhood education demonstration center.[35] Eighty-one schools submitted proposals; from these 81, ten were selected. The ten centers, enrolling 720 children, were housed in the following schools:

1. C. G. White School
   Powellsville, North Carolina
2. Aurelian Springs Elementary School
   Littleton, North Carolina
3. Brogden Elementary School
   Dudley, North Carolina
4. Walker Elementary School
   Fayetteville, North Carolina
5. Chadbourn Elementary School
   Chadbourn, North Carolina
6. Henry Grove Primary School
   Lilesville, North Carolina
7. North Elementary School
   Winston-Salem, North Carolina
8. Mountain View Elementary School
   Hays, North Carolina
9. Forest City Elementary School
   Forest City, North Carolina
10. Claxton Elementary School
    Asheville, North Carolina[36]

Learning Institute of North Carolina Evaluation

An evaluation of the kindergarten experiences was included as a part of the state program. The State Board of Education directed that the evaluation be planned cooperatively by the Learning Institute of North Carolina and the State Department of Public Instruction.

The 320 children who attended the Demonstration Centers were tested in December, 1969. Sixty-two children not attending the program were also tested at that date, but all 382 children were posttested in May, 1970.

The Tests of Basic Experiences (TOBE), published by the California Test Bureau, were administered to the control group and to the experimental group. The four subject matter areas tested were language, social studies, mathematics, and science. The following chart shows the comparison of the percentile values of the two groups:

	Language	Social Studies	Mathematics	Science
Kindergarten Children	64th	67th	59th	65th
Control Group	34th	39th	34th	40th [37]

54

Another test, the Cooperative Preschool Inventory (testing perceptual-motor skills, number concepts, vocabulary, and the ability to follow directions) showed that the kindergarten experiences had been profitable for the children. Of a possible 64 points, the pretest average score for the 320 kindergarten children who attended school was 46 points, and their posttest average score was 57. The average score for the control group children was 52 in the pretest and 48 in the posttest.

The Harris-Goodenough Draw-A-Man Test was used as an additional evaluation instrument. This test provided information concerning the mental age of the children. For the 320 children attending kindergarten, the mental age equivalent in December, 1969, was 5 years 1 month. After five months in kindergarten, the children were retested, and in May, 1970, the mental age was 5 years 11 months. Data to determine the mental age equivalent of the control group were not obtained in December, but test results indicated the mental age equivalent as 5 years 8 months when tested in May.[39]

To help evaluate the effects of kindergarten on children, the State Department of Public Instruction sent a questionnaire to the parents of the children attending the Demonstration Centers. The parents were asked, "Do you recommend that the State of North Carolina spend the necessary money to provide this kind of experience for all five-year-olds?" Of the 130 responses, two parents answered "No," one parent was undecided, and 127 answered "Yes."[40]

Some parents commented on the improvement of their children after attending kindergarten. Examples of some of the comments are as follows:

If this kindergarten could help other five-year-olds as our child has been helped, it will be more than worthwhile to continue this program.

This has definitely been a wonderful experience for my child. I feel he is ready to start first grade work. He understands what is expected of him as one of the group. He knows what it is to work on a schedule and routine. He has discovered that it's fun to learn and I think he is eager to learn. I do hope that soon all five-year-olds will be given the opportunity of this experience.[41]

The evaluations conducted by the Learning Institute of North Carolina seemed to indicate that the kindergarten program in North Carolina had a positive effect on children in relation to their school achievement. On the basis of the test scores reported, one could anticipate that the children participating in the kindergarten programs as they were set up had gained experiences which could be helpful to them in their achievement in school.

Summary

The Governor's Study Commission on the Public School System in North Carolina reported its findings to the General Assembly in 1969. The Commission gave priority to the establishment of a state-wide kindergarten program and recommended that public education be extended downward to include kindergarten as a regular part of the educational sequence of the public schools.

The Commission also recommended that certification requirements for teachers of young children be changed. The Commission suggested that more emphasis be placed on courses in growth and development of children between the ages of five and eight. The Division of Teacher Education of the State Department of Public Instruction acted upon the suggestion and the primary certificate was changed to Early Childhood Education Certificate.

In order for kindergartens to become a part of the public school system of North Carolina, legislation had to be enacted by the General Assembly. Senate Bill 109, passed in 1969, called "An Act to Authorize the State Board of Education to Establish a Kindergarten Program for Five-Year-Olds," provided the legal means to establish a public kindergarten program in North Carolina. The State Department of Public Instruction, with an appropriation of $1 million, began organizing and supervising the establishment of the kindergarten program.

Training for the personnel involved in the state kindergarten program was provided by the Kindergarten-Early Childhood Division of the State Department of Public Instruction and the Learning Institute of North Carolina. In the summer of 1969 a workshop was held at Tufts University, and in the summer of 1970 two institutes were held, one in the western and one in the eastern part of the state of North Carolina.

Eight demonstration centers were opened at a formal ceremony in December, 1969, and the kindergarten program was set up as a part of the public school system in North Carolina. The teachers employed to work with the 320 children who were enrolled in the kindergarten program were to be thought of as guides and resource people in the active process of working with young children. Ten more centers were opened in the state in the 1970-71 academic year.

According to the evaluation completed by the Learning Institute of North Carolina and the State Department of Public Instruction, the first year of the kindergarten program was a success in terms of test scores and parental evaluation. The children were tested at the beginning of their kindergarten experience and posttested five months later. The testing program indicated that the kindergarten program in North Carolina provided five-year-olds with experiences that tended to lead to school success.

CHAPTER V

CONCLUDING SUMMARY

Prior to 1940, public and private efforts to provide schools for young children were evident in North Carolina. As early as 1840, the General Assembly of North Carolina passed an act that stated that all white children under the age of 21 could go to school and receive instruction. Taken at face value, five-year-old children in the state could legally have been able to be a part of a public school system. No evidence was uncovered during the research for this book that revealed that five-year-old children attended school at public expense as a result of the 1840 law.

No action by the General Assembly was necessary for the establishment of private schools in the state. As for public schools, in 1923, the General Assembly enacted legislation that stated that any school district in the state could establish public kindergartens by a vote of the people in the district. During the period prior to 1940 no other legislation was enacted concerning public kindergartens in North Carolina.

Newspaper accounts reported that the Infant Schools were one of the earliest forms of formal education for young children in North Carolina. The Infant Schools were privately operated and purported to provide the children with the kinds of experiences that would enhance future learning. Infant Schools were in operation in North Carolina in the 1830's in the towns of Fayetteville and Raleigh.

The University of North Carolina introduced instruction in kindergarten methods into North Carolina in 1878. The University of North Carolina continued for several years to provide kindergarten instruction in the Normal School. Trinity College also offered courses in kindergarten work in 1878 under the direction of two kindergartners from Washington, D. C. The University of North Carolina session opened only two days prior to the Trinity College session.

Before 1940 several state normal schools in North Carolina, in addition to the University of North Carolina, offered courses in kindergarten instruction. In 1881, Franklin Normal School and Newton Normal School provided work in kindergarten methods. Asheville Normal School offered kindergarten instruction in the summer of 1885, as did Washington Normal School in 1888. An examination of the Reports of the Superintendent of Public Instruction for the years 1854 to 1971 indicated that kindergarten instruction in the normal schools was provided only for the years 1881, 1885, and 1888.

In the 1880s Peace Institute in Raleigh provided courses in kindergarten instruction for future teachers. As a part of

the course of study, a model school was provided in order
that the teachers might have a place to practice skills of
teaching. The Reverend Burwell was principal of the Institute,
in which the kindergarten children were taught spelling,
arithmetic, music, and art. The desks and chairs used by the
children were personally constructed by Burwell and were
designed to be especially useful to five-year-old children.

The North Carolina Institute for the Deaf and Dumb
and the Blind began to provide kindergarten experiences as part
of their program in 1892, when the need to develop the mind
and body of blind children was considered as important as
such development for sighted children. The school has continued
to maintain a class for five-year-old children.

In the early 1900's St. Paul's School in Beaufort maintained a kindergarten normal department. The aim of the training school was to prepare women for positions in kindergartens
as teachers or principals, and to better prepare women in
caring for young children. At the end of two years' work at
the training school, which included both academic courses and
practical experiences, the students completed the requirements
to become kindergartners.

Although the researcher was unable to find a great deal
of information on the subject, several mills in North Carolina
provided kindergartens for the children of their employees.
According to the United States Bureau of Education, in 1914
three mills in North Carolina, Proximity Manufacturing Company
in Greensboro, Jennings Cotton Mill in Lumberton, and Delagodo
Mills in Wilmington, offered kindergarten experiences for the
children of parents employed in the mills. John H. Cook
studied the mill school situation in North Carolina in 1925
and recommended that well-organized kindergartens be established
in the mills in North Carolina.

Only two public school systems in North Carolina operated
kindergartens prior to 1940. The Asheville city schools received
kindergarten buildings and equipment as a gift from the Asheville
Free Kindergarten Association in 1907. The General Assembly
of North Carolina enacted legislation that allowed the Asheville
public school system to accept the kindergartens in 1907, and
each year thereafter the system increased the number of schools
for pre-first grade children. Edmonds reported in her master's
thesis in 1929 that the Asheville public school system was
maintaining ten kindergartens. The kindergartens were terminated
in 1930, when the Attorney General of North Carolina, Dennis
Brummitt, ruled the kindergarens illegal since there had been
no vote of the people in the district to maintain such schools.

The second public school system in North Carolina to
operate a kindergarten prior to 1940 was the Washington public
schools. The kindergarten program in the Washington city schools
was begun in 1910. According to an article in North Carolina
Education in October, 1910, the kindergarten was considered
a success and carried the support of the school board, the

superintendent of schools and the school patrons. Although the program enjoyed success for a five-year period, the kindergarten was terminated in 1915 when the Washington Board of Education decided to place more emphasis on the domestic science department of the public school system.

Two school-related organizations expressed interest in public kindergartens prior to 1940. These organizations were the North Carolina Kindergarten Association and the North Carolina Congress of Parents and Teachers. The North Carolina Kindergarten Association was associated with the North Carolina Teachers Assembly and periodically provided programs for its members. Generally speaking, when the meetings were held the organizations seemed to attract persons of some national note as guest speakers. Annie E. George, Lucy Gage, and Ella Victoria Dobbs were among those leaders in work with young children who participated in the North Carolina Kindergarten Association meetings in the decade of the 1910's. In addition, interest was stimulated to such a degree that North Carolina Education published a monthly feature from 1910-12 entitled "Our Kindergarten Exchange" for the purpose of sharing ideas among educators in the state concerned with the education of young children. During the academic year 1923-24, the journal also published a monthly feature entitled "Kindergarten Department."

From the national level, two people offered encouragement to State Superintendent E. C. Brooks to provide kindergartens for the children of North Carolina. Nina C. Vandewalker, specialist in kindergarten education in the Bureau of Education in Washington, D. C., sent Brooks a letter in which she noted the status of kindergartens in the states of the Union in 1921, and expressed the desire that growth in public kindergarten education would extend to North Carolina. Bessie Locke, corresponding secretary for the National Kindergarten Association, based in New York City, noting a recent article by Brooks in which he had stated that North Carolina was to launch a campaign to increase the number of school buildings in the state, expressed the hope that these new buildings would all contain kindergarten classrooms. Locke also offered to send, free of charge if necessary, National Kindergarten Association leaflets that would provide additional information about kindergartens.

The State Normal and Industrial School in Greensboro (later Woman's College of the University of North Carolina, then the University of North Carolina at Greensboro) was established in 1891 by an act of the General Assembly. According to the catalogues of the school, the first kindergarten instruction was offered through a practice and observation school which opened in October, 1893, and enrolled children from five to eights years of age. The following year, the President of the State Normal and Industrial School, Charles D. McIver, placed an advertisement in the Greensboro Record which noted that the school was for children from the ages six to nine and would include grades 1 to 3. Apparently McIver was not completely satisfied with the primary school arrangement and in the Report of the Superintendent of Public Instruction, 1894-96, recommended that a kindergarten department be established for children between the ages of four and six. There is no evidence that the recommendation was accepted; however, in September, 1935, a kindergarten was established at Woman's College. The kindergarten continued to function as a practice and observation experience for the students enrolled in the College until 1970, when the kindergarten was terminated.

For the period of time from 1940 to 1968, a marked increase in interest in schools for young children occurred. Legally, the State Department of Public Instruction was assigned authority to supervise public and private kindergartens in the state, and a person with a degree in early childhood education was employed by the State Department of Public Instruction to assist in the supervision. For every session of the General Assembly from 1963 to 1967, bills were introduced that would have initiated a public kindergarten program in North Carolina, but each bill was defeated.

In 1948, East Carolina Teachers College (now East Carolina University) opened a kindergarten for the purpose of allowing students to observe kindergarten methods and to practice their skills of teaching. The kindergarten is still in operation and is providing practical experiences for students majoring in early childhood education.

In the period from 1940 to 1968 school-related organizations continued to advocate public kindergartens. The North Carolina Congress of Parents and Teachers continued its support, which had begun in 1920, of kindergartens as a part of the public school system of North Carolina. In addition, the North Carolina Congress provided pre-school services in order to assist parents of children who would soon enter first grade. The North Carolina Education Association and the North Carolina Teachers Association both endorsed public kindergartens, the former beginning in 1956 and the latter beginning in 1963, and each year the organizations continued their interest and support of public kindergartens. When the two associations merged in 1970, endorsement of public kindergartens remained a part of the legislative program of the newly formed North Carolina Association of Educators.

Two public school systems in North Carolina were involved in projects that provided kindergartens for a portion of the eliigible five-year-olds. In 1963, kindergartens were operated in two Orange County public schools as a section of a larger study of the rural South. The kindergartens were discontinued in 1965. In 1968, the Roanoke Rapids Graded School District established kindergartens as a part of the public school system, thereby operating the first public kindergartens in the state since the Asheville schools.

In the mid-1960's, North Carolina became a part of the network of states to participate in various federal programs and foundation programs on behalf of young children. Head Start served a number of children in the state, and the Elementary and Secondary Education Act, Title I, assisted in providing young children with experiences designed to enhance the chances of school success. The Summer Readiness Program of the Comprehensive School Improvement Project, a program jointly funded by the Ford Foundation and the State Department of Public Instruction, provided experiences that attempted to assure future educational successes for the children involved in the project.

By act of the 1967 General Assembly a Commission was created to study the public school system of North Carolina, and the findings of the study were to be presented to the General Assembly in 1969. The Commission gave top priority to a downward extension of the public school system to include a kindergarten program. Senate Bill 109, enacted in July, 1969, gave the legal means to provide a kindergarten program for five-year-olds in North Carolina.

After legal authority to establish kindergatens had been granted to the State Board of Education with an appropriation of $1 million, proposals from various school systems in the state were submitted in an effort to obtain a kindergarten for the district. Eight school systems were selected to establish Demonstration Centers that were to become the first state-supported kindergartens. The centers conducted programs for five-year-old children in the school system. They also served as demonstration centers for person interested in the educational and social aspects of the program.

Several institutes were conducted in the summer of 1969 in order to prepare personnel to assist in the organization and administration of the kindergarten program. By December of the same year, the kindergartens were ready to accept children, and 320 enrolled. Flexibility was a key word in the program, and the concept of using learning centers was at the core of the work to be done with the children. Individualized instruction, multi-age grouping, and team teaching were employed in an attempt to provide for the continuous progress of the children in the program.

In 1970, the State Board of Education directed that ten additonal centers be established for the school year 1970-71. For that school year, 720 children enrolled in the program, and for the 1969-71 biennium the early childhood demonstration centers were serving approximately one thousand five-year-olds in North Carolina.

From data gathered from pretests administered to the children in 1970 and posttests administered in 1971, the Learning Institute of North Carolina concluded that the first year of the kindergarten program was successful in terms of school success. Scores revealed that the children who attended the kindergarten program consistently performed better on several tests than did the children in the control group.

By 1971, kindergartens as a part of the public school system in North Carolina were well established. Continued growth in early childhood education for children in the state seemed inevitable.

FOOTNOTES

CHAPTER I

1. Robert H. Quick, <u>Essays on Educational Reformers</u> (New York: D. Appleton & Co., 1890), p. 394.

2. <u>Ibid</u>., p. 388

3. Evelyn Weber, <u>The Kindergarten: Its Encounter with Educational Thought in America</u> (New York: Teachers College Press, 1969), p. 12, compiled from Frederick Froebel, <u>The Education of Man</u>, trans. William N. Hailmann (New York: D. Appleton & Co., 1887), pp. 285-288.

4. Quick, <u>Essays on Educational Reformers</u>, p. 395.

5. Elizabeth Jenkins, "How the Kindergarten Found Its Way to America," <u>Wisconsin Magazine of History</u>, XIV (September, 1930), 52.

6. Elizabeth Peabody, "The Origins and Growth of the Kindergarten," <u>Education</u>, II (May, 1882), 523.

7. Evelyn Weber, <u>The Kindergarten</u>, pp. 27-33

8. <u>Rationale, Goals, and Plans for the Improvement of Education in North Carolina</u> (Raleigh: State Department of Public Instruction, 1970), p. 22.

9. <u>Ibid</u>.

CHAPTER II

1. State of North Carolina, <u>Laws of North Carolina, 1840-1841</u> (Raleigh: W. R. Gales, 1841), p. 15.

2. State of North Carolina, <u>Supplement to the Consolidated Statutes of North Carolina</u> (Raleigh: Edwards and Broughton Printing Co., 1924), p. 361.

3. State of North Carolina, <u>Private Laws of the State of North Carolina, 1907</u> (Raleigh: E. M. Uzzell & Co., State Printers and Binders, 1907), p. 421.

4. State of North Carolina, <u>The General Statutes of North Carolina</u>, Volume 3A (Charlottesville: The Michie Co., Law Publishers, 1966), p. 615.

5. John S. Brubacher, <u>A History of the Problems of Education</u> (2nd ed.; New York: McGraw-Hill, Inc., 1966), p. 381.

6. <u>Ibid</u>.

7. <u>Ibid</u>., pp. 368-369.

8. <u>Ibid</u>., p. 369.

9. Newton Edwards and Herman G. Richey, <u>The School in the American Social Order</u> (Boston: Houghton Mifflin Co., 1947), p. 264.

10. <u>Ibid</u>., p. 265.

11. "Infant Schools," <u>Raleigh Register</u>, September 23, 1830, p. 2.

Chapter II (continued)

12. *Ibid.*
13. *Ibid.*
14. "Infant School," *Carolina Observer*, January 4, 1832, p. 3.
15. "The Infant School," *North Carolina Standard*, January 12, 1842, p.2.
16. Brubacher, *A History of the Problems of Education*, p. 381.
17. *Catalogue of the Trustees, Visiters (sic), Faculty and Students, of Normal College, Randolph County, North Carolina, 1850-1851* (Salisbury: Carolina Watchman Office, 1851), p. 13.
18. *Catalogue of the Trustees, Visitors, Faculty and Students, of Normal College, Randolph County, North Carolina, 1851-1852* (Greensboro: Samuel W. James, 1852), p. 26.
19. *Catalogue of the Trustees, Faculty and Students of Normal College, Randolph County, North Carolina, 1852-1853* (Salisbury: Miller & James, Printers, 1853), p. 14.
20. *Ibid.*, p. 15.
21. *Catalogue of the Trustees, Faculty and Students of Normal College, Randolph County, North Carolina, 1850-1851,* p. 14; *1851-1852*, p. 27; *1852-1853*, p. 24; *1853-1854*, p. 22; *1854-1855*, p. 14.
22. "Trinity College Items," *Raleigh Christian Advocate*, February 6, 1878, p. 2.
23. "Trinity Normal School," *Raleigh Christian Advocate*, April 17, 1878, p. 2.
24. *Ibid.*, July 24, 1878, p. 2.
25. *Ibid.*
26. *Ibid.*
27. Department of Interior, *Report of the Commissioner of Education, 1874*, p. 578.
28. *Raleigh Christian Advocate*, July 24, 1878, p. 2.
29. Sidney Ann Wilson, "The History of Peace College, 1858-1890" (unpublished manuscript, Peace College, 1962), p.24.
30. *Circular and Catalogue of the Trustees, Instructors and Pupils of Peace Institute for Young Ladies* (Raleigh: Uzzell and Wiley, Printers and Binders, 1880), p. 5.
31. Emily Coe will be discussed in more detail *infra* (see pp. 18-19).
32. *Circular and Catalogue of the Trustees, Instructors and Pupils of Peace Institute*, p. 12.
33. *Ibid.*
34. *Ibid.*, p. 32.
35. *Circular and Catalogue of the Trustees, Instructors and Pupils of Peace Institute for Young Ladies, 1879-1889.*

Footnotes

Chapter II (Continued)

36. Fourteenth Annual Catalogue of Peace Institute for Young Ladies, 1885-1886 (Raleigh: Edwards and Broughton Co., Printers and Binders, 1886), p. 33.

37. Seventeenth Annual Catalogue of Peace Institute for Young Ladies, 1888-1889 (Raleigh: E. M. Uzzell, Steam Printers and Binders, 1889), p. 10.

38. George Huntley, III, "Nannie Geffroy Revived, Developed St. Paul's School," Cartaret County News Times, May 17, 1960, p.4.

39. Ibid.

40. Ibid.

41. Ibid; ibid., May 24, 1960, p. 4.

42. Carteret County News Times, May 24, 1960, p. 4.

43. Telephone conversation, George Huntley, III, descendant of Nannie Geffroy, January 11, 1973, and January 25, 1973.

44. Kindergarten Normal Department, St. Paul's School (Beaufort: Printing Department of St. Paul's School, n.d.), p.3.

45. Ibid., p. 5.

46. Ibid., p. 6.

47. Ibid., p.2.

48. Ibid., pp. 2-3.

49. In Kemp P. Battle, History of the University of North Carolina, 1868-1912 (Raleigh: Edwards and Broughton Printing Co., 1912), II, 603, Miss Johnson is listed as being from the Beaufort Training School.

50. Kindergarten Normal Department, St. Paul's School, pp. 9-10.

51. Biennial Report of the Superintendent of North Carolina, 1912-1914 (Raleigh: State Department of Public Instruction, 1915) p. 28.

52. Kindergartens in the United States (Washington, D.C.: Bureau of Education, 1914), p. 76.

53. Ibid.

54. Ibid.

55. Ibid.

56. John H. Cook, A Study of the Mill Schools of North Carolina (New York: Teachers College, 1925), p. 52.

57. Battle, History of the University of North Carolina, II, 157.

58. Ibid., p. 161.

59. Ibid., p. 158.

60. Department of Interior, Biennial Report of the Commissioner of Education, p. 576.

61. Catalogue of the University of North Carolina at Chapel Hill, 1878-1879 (Raleigh: Uzzell and Wiley, Printers and Binders, 1879), p. 49.

Chapter II (Continued)

62. Ibid., pp. 47-50.
63. Battle, History of the University of North Carolina, II, 162.
64. Ibid., p. 158.
65. Ibid., pp. 158-160.
66. Catalogue of the University of North Carolina at Chapel Hill, 1878-1879, p. 159.
67. Battle, History of the University of North Carolina, II, 186.
68. Ibid., p. 188.
69. Ibid., p. 187.
70. Catalogue of the University of North Carolina at Chapel Hill, 1880-1881 (Raleigh: Edwards, Broughton & Co., Printers and Binders, 1881), p. 50.
71. Biennial Report of the Superintendent of Public Instruction (Raleigh: P. M. Hale and Edwards, Broughton & Co., 1880), p. 19.
72. Catalogue of the University of North Carolina at Chapel Hill, Eighty-Seventh Year, 1881-1882 (Raleigh: Uzzell & Wiley, Steam Printers & Binders, 1882), p. 41.
73. Catalogue of the University of North Carolina at Chapel Hill, Eighty-Eighth Year, 1882-1884 (Raleigh: Edwards, Broughton & Co., Steam Printers & Binders, 1884), p. 29.
74. The University of North Carolina Catalogue, 1898-1899 (Chapel Hill: The University Press, 1899), p. 103.
75. Ibid.
76. Battle, History of the University of North Carolina, II, 603.
77. Ibid.
78. "The Normal School at Franklin, Macon County, North Carolina," North Carolina Educational Journal, I (August 15, 1881), 59.
79. Ibid.
80. Biennial Report of the Superintendent of Public Instruction, 1885-1886 (Raleigh: State Department of Public Instruction, 1887), p. 49.
81. Biennial Report of the Superintendent of Public Instruction, 1887-1888 (Raleigh: State Department of Public Instruction, 1889), p. 20.
82. Report of the North Carolina Institute for the Education of the Deaf and Dumb and the Blind, 1892-1894 (Raleigh: Guy V. Barnes, Printers to State Council, 1894), p. 29.
83. Ibid., p. 2.
84. Report of the North Carolina Institute for the Education of the Deaf and Dumb and the Blind, 1902-1904 (Raleigh: E. M. Uzzell, 1904), pp. 10-11.

Footnotes

Chapter II   (Continued)

85. Telephone conversation, John Calloway, Principal of the Governor Morehead School for the Blind and Deaf, January 4, 1972.

86: Minutes of the Meetings of the School Committee of Asheville, January, 1906, to June 22, 1909, p. 78.

87. Ibid., p. 100.

88. Private Laws of the State of North Carolina, 1907 (Raleigh: E. M. Uzzell State Printers and Binders, 1907), p. 420.

89. Ibid., p. 421

90. Minutes of the Meetings of the School Committee of Asheville, January, 1906, to June 22, 1909, p. 112.

91. Report of the Nineteenth to the Twenty-Second Years of the Public Schools of Asheville, p. 35.

92. Minutes of the Meetings of the School Committee of Asheville, July 9, 1909, to July 6, 1912, p. 65.

93. Edna D. Edmonds, "Provisions for Kindergarten Training in North Carolina" (unpublished master's thesis, University of North Carolina, 1929), p. 10.

94. Minutes of the Meetings of the School Committee of Asheville, July 9, 1909, to July 6, 1913, p. 165.

95. Report of the Twenty-third and Twenty-fourth Years of the Public Schools of Asheville, p. 9.

96. Minutes of the Meetings of the School Committee of Asheville, July 9, 1909, to July 6, 1912, p. 75.

97. Asheville Advocate, April 25, 1930, no pagination.

98. The Asheville Citizen, July 6, 1930, no pagination.

99. Conversation with Adrian Newton, Clerk of the Supreme Court of North Carolina, and Raymond Taylor, Marshal and Librarian of the Supreme Court of North Carolina, January 11, 1973.

100. "Submission of Controversy Without Action," in Robert E. Posey et al. v. Board of Education of Buncombe County et al., in the Supreme Court of North Carolina, Buncombe County, No. 607J (1930), p. 2.

101. Ibid., p. 6.

102. Ibid., p. 9.

103. Posey et al. v. Board of Education of Buncombe County et al., 199 N. C. 306, at pp. 311-312.

104. Ibid., at pp. 312-313.

105. Ibid., p. 313.

106. Association for Childhood Education, The History of the Kindergarten Movement of the Southeastern States (n.p.: Association for Childhood Education, 1939), p. 34.

107. Twelfth Annual Report of the Public Schools of the City of Washington, North Carolina, July 1, 1908-June 30, 1909 (Raleigh: Edwards and Broughton Printing Co., 1909), pp. 42-43.

Chapter II (continued)

108. Ibid., p. 43.
109. "Washington Kindergarten Opens with 51 Pupils,"
North Carolina Education, IV (October, 1910), p. 19.
110. Thirteenth Annual Report of the Public Schools of
the City of Washington, North Carolina, July 1, 1909-June 30,
1910 (Washington, N.C.: Tidewater Printing Co., 1910), p. 39.
111. Ibid.
112. Minutes of the Board of School Trustees of the Town
of Washington, Book I, May 26, 1915, no pagination.
113. Program of the North Carolina Teachers Assembly,
Twenty-first Annual Session, June 8-12, 1904, p. 3.
114. "N.C.K.A. Organized," North Carolina Education, VI
(January, 1912), 28-29.
115. "Kindergarten Teachers," North Carolina Education,
VI (December, 1912), 4.
116. "Our Kindergarten Exchange," North Carolina Education,
no volume number given (May, 1910), p. 20; ibid. (June, 1910),
p. 15; ibid. (September, 1910), p. 10; ibid., IV (February, 1912),
6-7; ibid. (April, 1912), p. 7; ibid., May, (1912), p. 8.
117. Letter, Hattie M. Scott to E. E. Sams, October 10, 1913,
North Carolina Department of Archives and History, Letter File,
Office of the Superintendent of Public Instruction.
118. Ibid., October 22, 1913.
119. Ibid., November 3, 1913.
120. North Carolina Education, X (November, 1915), 16.
121. Ibid., XVII (March, 1923), 13.
122. "Kindergarten Department," North Carolina Education,
XVII (May, 1923), 6-7; (September, 1923), pp. 10-11; (October, 1923),
p. 7; (November, 1923), p. 5; (January, 1924), p. 16: (February,
1924), p. 15; (March, 1924), p. 13; (June, 1924), p. 9.
123. Program of the Fourteenth Annual Session of the North
Carolina Education Association, Raleigh, March 12-14, 1924,
p. 12.
124. Minutes and Records of the North Carolina Congress of
Parents and Teachers, vol. I, 1919-1930, p. 5.
125. Thad Stem, PTA Impact: 50 Years in North Carolina, 1919-
1969 (Raleigh: North Carolina Congress of Parents and Teachers,
Inc., 1969), pp. 6-7.
126. Ibid., p. 84.
127. North Carolina Congress of Parents and Teachers,
Proceedings, 1936-1971, p. 22.
128. Letter, Nina C. Vandewalker to E. C. Brooks, July 14,
1921, North Carolina Department of Archives and History, Letter
File, Office of the Superintendent of Public Instruction.

Chapter II   (Continued)

129.   Letter, Bessie Locke to E. C. Brooks, June 21, 1921, North Carolina Department of Archives and History, Letter File, Office of the Superintendent of Public Instruction.

130.   Letter, E. C. Brooks to Bessie Locke, July 14, 1921, North Carolina Department of Archives and History, Letter File, Office of the Superintendent of Public Instruction.

131.   First Annual Catalog of the State Normal and Industrial School, 1892-93 (Greensboro: C. F. Thomas, Printer, 1894), p. 14.

132.   Second Annual Catalogue of the State Normal and Industrial School, 1893-94 (Greensboro: C. F. Thomas, Printer, 1895), p. 23.

133.   Ibid.

134.   Ibid.

135.   Elizabeth Bowles, A Good Beginning: The First Four Decades of the University of North Carolina at Greensboro (Chapel Hill: The University of North Carolina Press, 1967), p. 95.   Bowles does not document her source other than to state that the information was found in the Greensboro Record, 1894. Inquiries to the North Carolina Department of Archives and History and to the Greensboro Record revealed that none of the Records for 1894 are on file.

136.   Report of the Superintendent of Public Instruction, 1894-1896 (Winston: M. I. and J. C. Stewart, 1897), p. 25.

137.   Telephone conversation, Eugenia Hunter, August 8, 1972.

138.   "Editorial," North Carolina Education, XVII (June, 1923), 12.

CHAPTER III

1.   State of North Carolina, Session Laws and Resolutions, 1945 General Assembly (Raleigh: Published by Authority), p. 1284.

2.   Letter, Patsy Montague, former supervisor, State Department of Public Instruction, March 13, 1971.

3.   Letter, Dr. Clyde Erwin from Assistant Attorney General Claude Love, Research and Information Center, State Department of Public Instruction, May 20, 1952.

4.   State of North Carolina, Session Laws and Resolutions, 1955 General Assembly (Raleigh: Published by Authority), p. 1543.

5.   House Bill 792 of the General Assembly of North Carolina, 1963 Session, pp. 1-5.

6.   Letter, Rebecca S. Ballentine, Librarian, Institute of Government, Chapel Hill, February 10, 1972.

7.   Daily Legislative Bulletin, No. 28, March 12, 1965, Chapel Hill: Institute of Government, no continuous pagination.

Footnotes

Chapter III (Continued)

    8. Letter, Rebecca S. Ballentine, February 10, 1972.

    9. Daily Legislative Bulletin, No. 2, February 9, 1967.
Chapel Hill: Institute of Government, no continuous pagination.

    10. Ibid., No. 32, March 23, 1967, p. 244.

    11. State of North Carolina, Session Laws and Resolutions,
1966 General Assembly (Raleigh: Published by Authority),
pp. 1981-82.

    12. Letter, Anne Rabe to Clyde Erwin, North Carolina
Department of Archives and History, Letter File, Office of the
Superintendent of Public Instruction, May 10, 1941.

    13. Letter, Patsy Montague, former supervisor, State
Department of Public Instruction, March 13, 1971.

    14. Ibid.

    15. Letter, Charlotte Barnes, Supervisor for non-public
kindergartens, State Department of Public Instruction, October 20,
1971.

    16. Biennial Report of the Superintendent of Public Instruc-
tion, 1950-52 (Raleigh: State Department of Public Instruction),
p. 104.

    17. Ibid.

    18. Ibid., 1952-54, p. 151.

    19. Ibid., 1954-56, p. 85; ibid., 1956-58, p. 88.

    20. Ibid., 1960-62, p. 101.

    21. Ibid., 1964-66, p. 139.

    22. Ibid., 1966-68, p. 128.

    23. Catalogue of East Carolina Teachers College, 1944-45,
p. 138.

    24. Ibid., 1945-46, p. 148; ibid., 1946-47, p. 136.

    25. Letter, Annie Mae Murray, first teacher at the East
Carolina College Kindergarten, June 19, 1972.

    26. Ibid.

    27. Ibid.

    28. Yearbook and Proceedings, 1946, pp. 58-59; ibid.,
1946-47, p. 73; ibid., 1948, p. 61; ibid., 1954, pp. 60-61;
ibid., 1960, p. 36.

    29. Stem, PTA Impact, p. 210.

    30. Ibid., p. 218.

    31. Yearbook and Proceedings, 1967-68, p. 73.

    32. Personal interview, Glenn Keever, editor of North
Carolina Education, Raleigh, May 19, 1972.

    33. "Legislative Survey," NCEA News Bulletin, XVI
(January, 1964), 3.

    34. Ibid., XX (January, 1968), 3.

    35. "Resolutions Adopted at the 82nd Annual Convention of
North Carolina Teachers Association, April 4-8, 1963," North
Carolina Teachers Record, XXXIII (May, 1963), 25.

Footnotes

Chapter III (Continued)

36. <u>North Carolina Teachers Record</u>, XXXIV (May, 1964), 19; <u>ibid</u>., XXXV (May, 1965), 15; <u>ibid</u>., XXXVI (May, 1966), 25; <u>ibid</u>., XXXVII (May, 1967), 21; <u>ibid</u>., XXXVIII (May, 1968), 18; <u>ibid</u>., XXXIX (May, 1969), 3.

37. Personal interview, E. B. Palmer, Associate Executive Secretary, North Carolina Association of Educators, Raleigh, January 10, 1973; telephone conversations with Ruth L. Woodson, Supervisor, Division of Kindergarten-Early Childhood Education, State Department of Public Instruction, Raleigh, January 12, 1973; with Dr. Alfonso Elder, President Emeritus, North Carolina Central University, February 9, 1973; and with Dr. Lewis Dowdy, President, A & T University, Greensboro, February 9, 1973.

38. Letter, G. P. Carr, Superintendent of Orange County Schools, to Charles F. Carroll, State Superintendent of Public Instruction, February 9, 1962.

39. Letter, Assistant Attorney General Ralph Moody to Superintendent Carr, February 23, 1962.

40. Letter, J. W. Talley, Superintendent of Roanoke Rapids Graded School District, January 8, 1971.

41. <u>Born A-Growing. A Summary Report of the North Carolina Comprehensive School Improvement Project, 1964-67</u> (Raleigh: State Department of Public Instruction, 1968), p. 1.

42. <u>Ibid</u>., p. 35.

43. <u>Ibid</u>.

44. <u>Ibid</u>., p. 3.

45. Jenny W. Klein, "Head Start: National Focus on Children," <u>National Elementary Principal</u>, LI (September, 1971), 99.

46. <u>Ibid</u>.

47. <u>Minutes of the State Board of Education</u>, April 1, 1965, XII, 260.

48. Klein, "Head Start," p. 99.

49. <u>Ibid</u>., p. 100.

50. Beatrice H. Criner, ed., <u>Directions for Title I, ESEA of 1965</u> (Raleigh: Title I, ESEA, State Department of Public Instruction, 1969), p. 2; <u>Minutes of the State Board of Education</u>, September 2, 1965, XII, 294.

51. Criner, <u>Directions for Title I, ESEA of 1965</u>, pp. 14-15.

52. Beatrice H. Criner, ed., <u>Off the Record, ESEA in 1967-1968</u> (Raleigh: Title I, ESEA, State Department of Public Instruction, 1969), p. 6.

53. Beatrice H. Criner, ed., "Bold Beginnings in North Carolina," <u>Benchmarks</u>, IV (December, 1969), 2.

CHAPTER IV

1. *Report of the Governor's Study Commission on the Public School System of North Carolina* (Raleigh: North Carolina State University Print Shop, 1968), p. 53.

2. *Ibid.*, p. 252.

3. *Ibid.*, p. 46.

4. *Ibid.*, p. 274.

5. *Ibid.*

6. *Ibid.*, p. 55.

7. State of North Carolina, *Session Laws and Resolutions*, 1969 General Assembly (Raleigh: Printed by Authority, 1970), p. 1401.

8. *Report of the Governor's Study Commission on the Public School System of North Carolina*, p. 56.

9. *Ibid.*

10. *Ibid.*, p. 60.

11. *Ibid.*, p. 57.

12. *Ibid.*, p. 181.

13. *Ibid.*, p. 182.

14. *Teaching in North Carolina* (Raleigh: State Department of Public Instruction, 1969), p. 12.

15. State of North Carolina, *Session Laws and Resolutions*, 1969 General Assembly (Raleigh: Printed by Authority), pp. 1400-01.

16. Letter, Martha Evans, former Senator of the General Assembly of North Carolina, August 18, 1971.

17. Letter, Robert W. Scott, Governor of North Carolina, June 2, 1972.

18. Learning Institute of North Carolina, "Kindergartens With a Future." Durham: 1970, p. 7. (Mimeographed.)

19. *Minutues of the State Board of Education*, XII (June 6, 1957-July 2, 1970), 541. (Typewritten.)

20. *Ibid.*

21. *Ibid.*, p. 544.

22. State Department of Public Instruction, "Nature and Status of Early Childhood Programs in North Carolina." Raleigh, 1969, pp. 1-2. (Mimeographed.)

23. Learning Institute of North Carolina, "Report on the Early Childhood Leadership Development Institute." Durham, 1970, p. 5. (Mimeographed.)

24. Letter, James W. Jenkins, Director, Early Childhood Education, State Department of Public Instruction, May 26, 1972.

25. Learning Institute of North Carolina, "Report on the Early Childhood Leadership Development Institute," pp. 2-5.

26. State Department of Public Instruction, "Plans for Kindergarten-Early Childhood Education Demonstration Center Ribbon-Cutting Ceremony," Raleigh, 1969, p. 1. (Mimeographed.)

Footnotes

Chapter IV   (Continued)

27.   State Department of Public Instruction, "Kindergartens-North Carolina's Pilot Effort," Raleigh, 1970, pp. 1-2. (Mimeographed.)
28.   J. W. Jenkins, "The North Carolina Approach to Kindergarten-Early Childhood Education," Raleigh, 1970, p. 3. (Mimeographed.)
29.   Ibid., p. 2.
30.   State Department of Public Instruction, "A Child Shall Lead Us," Raleigh, 1970, p. 4.   (Mimeographed.)
31.   "Kindergartens with a Future," pp. 2-3.
32.   Jenkins,   "The North Carolina Approach to Kindergarten-Early Childhood Education," pp.5-6.
33.   "Kindergartens with a Future," p. 3.
34.   Letter, James W. Jenkins, May 26, 1972.
35.   "Kindergartens with a Future," p. 10.
36.   Betty Landsberger, "Kindergarten Evaluation," North Carolina Public Schools, XXXV (Winter, 1970), 6.
37.   Ibid.
38.   Ibid.
39.   Suzanne Triplett, Learning Institute of North Carolina, telephone conversation, February 27, 1973.
40.   Landsberger, "Kindergarten Evaluation," p. 7.
41.   Ibid.

SELECTED BIBLIOGRAPHY

Books

Association for Childhood Education International. <u>Dauntless Women in Childhood Education, 1856-1931</u>. Washington, D.C.: Association for Childhood Education International, 1972.

Barnard, Henry, ed. <u>Kindergarten and Child Culture Papers</u>. Hartford, Conn.: Office of Barnard's American Journal of Education, 1890.

Battle, Kemp P. <u>History of the University of North Carolina, 1868-1912</u>. Vol. II. Raleigh: Edwards and Broughton Printing Co., 1912.

Bowles, Elizabeth Ann. <u>A Good Beginning: The First Four Decades of the University of North Carolina at Greensboro</u>. Chapel Hill: University of North Carolina Press, 1967.

Brubacher, John W. <u>A History of the Problems of Education</u>. 2nd ed. New York: McGraw-Hill, Inc., 1966.

Butts, R. Freeman. <u>A Cultural History of Western Europe</u>. New York: McGraw-Hill Book Co., Inc., 1955.

Cook, John Harrison. <u>A Study of the Mill Schools of North Carolina</u>. New York: Teachers College, 1925.

Coon, Charles L. <u>The Beginnings of Public Education in North Carolina: A Documentary History 1790-1840</u>. Raleigh: Edwards and Broughton Printing Co., 1908.

_____. <u>North Carolina Schools and Academies: A Documentary History, 1790-1840</u>. Raleigh: Edwards and Broughton Printing Co., 1915.

Dahlstrom, William G., and Baughman, Emmett E. <u>Negro and White Children: A Psychological Study in the Rural South</u>. New York: Academic Press, 1968.

Edwards, Newton, and Richey, Herman G. <u>The School in the American Social Order</u>. Boston: Houghton-Mifflin Co., 1947.

Forest, Ilse. <u>Preschool Education: A Historical and Critical Study</u>. New York: The Macmillan Co., 1927.

Froebel, Frederick. <u>The Education of Man</u>. Translated by William N. Hailmann. New York: D. Appleton & Co., 1887.

Headley, Neith. *The Kindergarten: Its Place in the Program of Education.* New York: The Center for Applied Research in Education, Inc., 1965.

Johnson, Guion Griffis. *Ante-Bellum North Carolina: A Social History.* Chapel Hill: University of North Carolina Press, 1937.

Knight, Edgar W. *A Documentary History of Education in the South Before 1860.* Chapel Hill: University of North Carolina Press, 1950.

_____. *Public School Education in North Carolina.* Boston: Houghton-Mifflin Co., 1916.

National Society for the Study of Education. *American Education in the Postwar Period: Curriculum Reconstruction.* Forty-Fourth Yearbook, Part I. Chicago: University of Chicago Press, 1948.

_____. *The Co-Ordination of the Kindergarten and the Elementary School.* Seventh Yearbook, Part II. Chicago: University of Chicago Press, 1908.

_____. *Early Childhood Education.* Forty-sixth Yearbook, Part II. Chicago: University of Chicago Press, 1956.

_____. *Early Childhood Education.* Seventy-first Yearbook, Part II. Chicago: University of Chicago Press, 1972.

_____. *The Kindergarten and Its Relation to Elementary Education.* Sixth Yearbook, Part II. Bloomington, Ill.: Public School Publishing Company, 1907.

Noble, Marcus C. S. *A History of the Public Schools of North Carolina.* Chapel Hill: University of North Carolina Press, 1930.

Painter, F.V.N. *A History of Education.* New York: D. Appleton & Co., 1886.

Parker, Samuel C., and Temple, Alice. *Unified Kindergarten and First-Grade Teaching.* New York: Ginn & Co., 1925.

Quick, Robert H. *Essays on Educational Reformers.* New York: D. Appleton & Co., 1890.

Raymont, Thomas. *A History of the Education of Young Children.* New York: Longmans, Green and Co., 1937.

Smith, Charles Lee. The History of Education in North Carolina. Washington, D.C.: Government Printing Office, 1888.

Stem, Thad. PTA Impact: 50 Years in North Carolina, 1919-
1969. Raleigh: North Carolina Congress of Parents and
Teachers, Inc., 1969.

Vandewalker, Nina C. The Kindergarten in American Education.
New York: Macmillan Co., 1908.

Weber, Evelyn. The Kindergarten: Its Encounter with Educational Thought in America. New York: Teachers College
Press, 1969.

Periodicals

Berson, Minnie P. "Early Childhood Education." American
Education, IV (October, 1968), 7-13.

Carr, William G. "The Status of the Kindergarten." Childhood
Education, X (March, 1934), 283-285,332.

"Constitution of the North Carolina State Kindergarten Association." North Carolina Education, XVII (June, 1923), 7-8.

Criner, Beatrice H., ed. "Bold Beginnings in North Carolina."
Benchmarks, IV (December, 1969), 2.

Davis, Mary Dabney. "A Century of Kindergarten." School
Life, XXII (November, 1936), 67-68.

_____. "The Listening Post." Educational Leadership, II
(November, 1944), 75.

Day, Barbara. "Getting Ready for Kindergarten." North
Carolina Education, XXXV (April, 1969), 14-15, 60-61.

Dean, Stuart E. "Education of Little Children--A Few Facts."
School Life, XLIII (February-March, 1961), 20.

Dunning, F.A.B. "Who is the Kindergartner?" North Carolina
Educational Journal, I (May 15, 1881), 35.

"Editorial." North Carolina Educational Journal, I (July 15,
1881), 52.

"Education." Popular Government, XXXVI (September, 1969),
39-48.

Furman, Helen A. "A North Carolina Report on Project Head Start." Reading Teacher, XIX (February, 1966), 342-346.

Gabbard, Hazel F. "A Nation's Concern for Kindergartens." School Life, XLI (May, 1959), 10-12.

Gage, Lucy. "The South's Interest in Kindergarten-Primary Education." Childhood Education, VI (September, 1929), 13-17.

Goodykoontz, Bess. "The Elementary School of Tomorrow--Its Possible Structure." Childhood Education, XXII (January, 1946), 215-220.

Headley, Neith. "The Kindergarten Comes of Age." NEA Journal, XLIII (March, 1954), 153-154.

"Is the Kindergarten the Remedy?" North Carolina Education, XVII (May, 1923), 11.

Jenkins, Elizabeth. "How the Kindergarten Found Its Way to America." Wisconsin Magazine of History, XLV (September, 1930), 48-62.

Jenkins, James W. "Changes Ahead: Are You Ready?" North Carolina Education, LXIII (March, 1969), 14-15.

_____. Interviewed by Glenn Keever. "How Now the Kindergarten Program?" North Carolina Education, I (October, 1970), 11-12, 36.

_____. "The Overall Picture of Kindergarten-Early Childhood Education in North Carolina." North Carolina Parent-Teacher Bulletin, XLIV (January, 1969), 8, 19.

_____. "The Overall Picture of Kindergarten-Early Childhood Education in North Carolina, Part II." North Carolina Parent-Teacher Bulletin, XLIV (February, 1969), 10-11.

Keever, Glenn. "A Child Well Taught." North Carolina Education, XXXV (January, 1969), 14-17.

Kiessel, William C., Jr. "The Kindergarten in America." Education, LXXV (April, 1955), 540-544.

"Kindergarten." North Carolina Educational Journal, I (February 15, 1881), 9.

"A Kindergarten Easter Service." North Carolina Education, XVIII (May, 1924), 19.

"Kindergarten Meetings at the State Association." North Carolina Education, XVIII (April, 1924), 4.

"Kindergarten Teachers." North Carolina Education, VI (December, 1912), 4.

"Kindergartens." North Carolina Educational Journal, II (June 20, 1882), 38.

"Kindergartens a Part of Asheville's Public Schools." North Carolina Education, XVII (May, 1923), 6.

Klein, Jenny W. "Head Start: National Focus on Young Children." National Elementary Principal, LI (September, 1971), 98-103.

Landsberger, Betty. "Kindergarten Evaluation." North Carolina Public Schools, XXXVI, No. 2 (Winter, 1970), 6-7.

Locke, Bessie. "Work of the National Kindergarten Association." North Carolina Education, IX (September, 1916), 15.

Montague, Patsy. "Kindergarten and First Grade Programs for Today." Educational Leadership, XVI (February, 1959), 292-295.

Murray, Annie Mae. "Make Way for Kindergartens." North Carolina Education, XIX (March, 1953), 22,67.

"N.C.K.A. Organized." North Carolina Education, VI (January,1912), 28-29.

"The Normal School of Franklin, Macon County, North Carolina." North Carolina Educational Journal, I (August 15, 1881), 59.

North Carolina Teachers Record. I (January, 1930)-XXXIX (May, 1969).

"Our Kindergarten Exchange." North Carolina Education, VI (February, 1912), 6-7; (March, 1912), p. 11; (April, 1912), p. 7; (May, 1912), p. 8.

Palmer, E. B. "It's Your 'Thing.' Do What You Want to do!" North Carolina Teachers Record, XXXIX (May, 1969), 3-4.

Peabody, Elizabeth. "The Origin and Growth of the Kindergarten."
  Education II (May, 1882), 507-527.

"Public Schools." *Popular Government*, XXXVIII (September, 1971),
  59-65.

"Resolutions Adopted at the Annual Convention of NCTA." *North
  Carolina Teachers Record*, XXXIII (May, 1963), 25.

"Some Effects of Kindergarten." *North Carolina Educational
  Journal*, II (March 15, 1882), 19.

Stockard, Marietta. "Froebel, the Founder of the Kindergarten."
  North Carolina Journal of Education, I (November 1, 1906),
  13.

_____. "The True Importance of the Kindergarten." *North
  Carolina Journal of Education*, I (September 15, 1906), 11.

Wharton, W. L. "The Kindergarten--What--Why--How." *North
  Carolina Parent-Teacher Bulletin*, XV (February, 1937), 9-10.

"What the Kindergarten is For." *North Carolina Education*, VII
  (November, 1912), 12.

Newspapers

"Asheville City Schools," *Asheville Citizen*, August 6, 1922.

"Committee Reports Study of State Kindergartens." *News and
  Observer*, October 7, 1962.

Early Childhood Education Newsletter. Raleigh: State Department
  of Public Insturction. Vol. I, No. 2. October, 1970.

Huntley, George, III. "Nannie Geffroy Revived, Developed St.
  Paul's School." *Carteret County News Times*, May 17, 1960.

_____. "Nannie Geffroy Revived, Developed St. Paul's School."
  Carteret County News Times, May 24, 1960.

"Infant School." *Carolina Observer*, January 4, 1832.

"The Infant School." *North Carolina Standard*, January 12, 1842.

"Infant Schools." *Raleigh Register*, September 23, 1830.

"Kindergarten and Colleges, Illegal." *Asheville Advocate*,
  April 25, 1930.

"Legislative Survey." NCEA News Bulletin, XVI (January, 1964), 1-4.

"Legislative Survey." NCEA News Bulletin, XX (January, 1968), 1-4.

"NCEA Legislative Goals." NCEA News Bulletin, XII (November, 1958), 1-4.

"NCEA Legislative Program Announced." NCEA News Bulletin, IX (March, 1956), 1-4.

"North Carolina Among Few Without Kindergartens." News and Observer, April 3, 1966.

"State Board, UFE Programs Compared." NCEA News Bulletin, XIX (November, 1966), 1-4.

"Trinity Normal School." Raleigh Christian Advocate, February 6, 18 April 17, 1878; July 24, 1878.

"UFE Asks 6,000-12,000 Salary Schedule." NCEA News Bulletin, XX (March, 1968), 1-4.

"UFE Program." NCEA News Bulletin, XVI (March, 1964), 1-4.

Legislative Journals, Laws, Reports, and Proceedings

Davis, Lucy T. ed. The Report of the Governor's Study Commission on the Public School System of North Carolina. Raleigh: North Carolina State University Print Shop, 1968.

Department of Interior. Report of the Commissioner of Education, 1867-1917.

North Carolina. The General Statutes of North Carolina, 1967.

_____. The General Statutes of North Carolina, 1969.

_____. Journal of the House of Representatives of the General Assembly of the State of North Carolina. Winston-Salem: Winston Printing Co., 1963.

North Carolina. Journal of the Senate of the General Assembly of the State of North Carolina, 1969.

_____. Laws of North Carolina, 1840-41.

_____. Private Laws of the State of North Carolina. Passed by the General Assembly 1907. Raleigh: E. M. Uzzell and Co., State Printers and Binders, 1907.

_____. _Public-Local and Private Laws of North Carolina_. 1900-1945.

_____. _The Public School Laws of North Carolina_. Codification of 1923. Raleigh: State Superintendent of Public Instruction, 1923.

_____. _Report of the North Carolina Institution for the Education of the Deaf and Dumb and the Blind_. 1892-93, 1894-96, 1896-98, 1898-1900, 1900-02, 1902-04, 1904-06, 1906-08, 1908-1910.

_____. _Revised Code of North Carolina, enacted by the General Assembly at the Session of 1854_. Boston: Little, Brown and Co., 1855.

_____. _Session Laws and Regulations, passed by the General Assembly at the Regular Session held in the city of Raleigh beginning on Wednesday, the fifth of January, A.D. 1955_. Published by authority.

_____. _Supplement to the Consolidated Statutes of North Carolina_. Raleigh: Edwards and Broughton Printing Co., 1924.

North Carolina Congress of Parents and Teachers. _Convention Programs_, 1949-1971.

_____. _Minutes and Records of the North Carolina Congress of Parents and Teachers_, 1919-1930.

_____. _Minutes and Records of the North Carolina Congress of Parents and Teachers, Inc._ Vol. VII, April, 1962-May, 1966. Raleigh: State PTA Office.

_____. _Proceedings_. Raleigh, North Carolina: North Carolina Congress of Parents and Teachers, 1936-1971.

North Carolina Department of Public Instruction. _Report of the Superintendent of Public Instruction_, 1854-1971.

North Carolina Education Association. _Convention Manuals and Programs_, 1954-1971.

_____. _Program, Fortieth Annual Session, North Carolina Education Association_, March 12-14, 1924.

North Carolina Teachers Assembly. _Proceedings and Addresses of the 31st Annual Session of the North Carolina Teachers Assembly_. November 25-28, 1914. Raleigh: State Superintendent of Public Instruction, 1915.

North Carolina Teachers Assembly. Program, 21st Annual Session, June 8-12, 1904.

Report of the Nineteenth to the Twenty-Second Years of the the Public Schools of Asheville, North Carolina, Ending July the Thirty-First, Nineteen Hundred and Nine. Asheville: Hackney and Moale Co., 1910.

Report of the Twenty-Third and Twenty-Fourth Years of the Public Schools of Asheville, North Carolina, Ending July 31st, 1911. Raleigh: Edwards and Broughton, 1912.

Thirteenth Annual Report of the Public Schools of the City of Washington, North Carolina, July 1, 1909-June 30, 1910. Washington, N. C.: Tidewater Printing Co., 1910.

Twelfth Annual Report of the Public Schools of the City of Washington, North Carolina, July 1, 1908-June 30, 1909. Raleigh: Edwards and Broughton Printing Co., 1909.

Yearbook of the City of Asheville, North Carolina, 1896-1897. Asheville: The Citizen Co., 1897.

Unpublished Material

Brown, George C. "History of Public Education in the City of Asheville, North Carolina." Unpublished Master's thesis. University of Maryland, 1940.

Davis, Anita Price. "The Comprehensive School Improvement Project in North Carolina." Unpublished Ph. D. dissertation, Duke University, 1971.

Edmonds, Edna D. "Provisions for Kindergarten Training in North Carolina." Unpublished Master's thesis, University of North Carolina, 1929.

James, Ruby Spainhour. "A Survey of the Status of Preprimary Schools in North Carolina." Unpublished Master's thesis, University of North Carolina, 1947.

Jenkins, J. W. "The North Carolina Approach to Kindergarten-Early Childhood Education." March, 1970. (Mimeographed.)

"Kindergarten Demonstration Centers Allocated by North Carolina
State Board of Education, March 2, 1970." Raleigh:
State Department of Public Instruction, 1970.
(Mimeographed.)

"Kindergarten-North Carolina's Pilot Effort." Raleigh:
State Department of Public Instruction, Early Childhood Education Division, 1970. (Mimeographed.)

"Kindergartens with a Future." Durham: Learning Institute
of North Carolina, November 19, 1970. (Mimeographed.)

Minutes of the Board of School Trustees of the Town of
Washington. Book I.

Minutes of the Meetings of the School Committee of Asheville,
January 1906-June 22, 1909; July 9, 1909-July 6, 1913.

Minutes of the State Board of Education. Vol. 11, July 30,
1934-May 2, 1957; vol. 12, June 6, 1957-July 2, 1970.

"Nature and Status of Early Childhood Programs in North Carolina."
Raleigh: State Department of Public Instruction, 1969.
(Mimeographed.)

"The Need for Public School Kindergartens." Raleigh: State
Department of Public Instruction, 1969. (Mimeographed.)

North Carolina Association for Childhood Education. "Kindergarten Study," 1962. (Mimeographed.)

_____. "Report: Nursery-Kindergarten Study Committee,"
April, 1964. (Mimeographed.)

The North Carolina State Board of Education Presents "A
Child Shall Lead Us." Raleigh: State Department of
Public Instruction, 1970. (Mimeographed.)

"Plans for Kindergarten-Early Childhood Education Demonstration
Center Ribbon-Cutting Ceremony." Raleigh: State Department of Public Instruction, 1969. (Mimeographed.)

Plemmons, William H. "The City of Asheville: Historical and
Institutional." Unpublished Master's thesis, Duke
University, 1935.

"Report on the Early Childhood Leadership Development Institute."
Durham: Learning Institute on North Carolina, 1970.
(Mimeographed.)

"A Statistical Report on Pre-Primary Education in The
Southern Region: 1970-71." Compiled by Therry
N. Deal. (Mimeographed.)

Wilson, Sidney Ann. "The History of Peace College,
1858-1890." Unpublished manuscript, 1962.

"Why Kindergartens?" Prepared for the Greensboro City
Board of Education by Subcommittee on Kindergartens,
March, 1967. (Mimeographed.)

Oral Communications

Calloway, John. Principal, Governor Morehead School for the
Blind and Deaf. Raleigh, January 4, 1972.

Dowdy, Lewis. President, A. & T. University, Greensboro,
February 9, 1973.

Elder, Alfonso. President Emeritus, North Carolina Central
University, Durham, February 9, 1973.

Hunter, Eugenia. Early Childhood Education, University of
North Carolina-Greensboro, Greensboro, August 8, 1972.

Huntley, George, III. Descendant of Nannie Geffroy, founder
of St. Paul's Kindergarten, January 11, 1973.

Jenkins, James W. Director, Division of Kindergarten-Early
Childhood Education, State Department of Public Instruction,
Raleigh, January 12, 1971, and June 17, 1971.

Keever, Glenn. Editor of North Carolina Education, Raleigh,
May 9, 1972.

Mason, John. Institute of Government, Chapel Hill, July 21,
1972.

Miller, J. Everette. Former Assistant Superintendent of Public
Instruction of North Carolina, Raleigh, January 10, 1971.

Murray Annie Mae. Professor of Education Emeritus, East
Carolina University, Charlotte, August 31, 1971.

Newton, Adrian. Clerk of the Supreme Court cf North Carolina,
Raleigh, January 11, 1973.

Palmer, E. B. Associate Executive Secretary of North Carolina Association of Educators, Raleigh, January 9, 1973.

Ray, Richard. Director, Learning Institute of North Carolina, Durham, January 27, 1971.

Taylor, J. Arthur. Assistant Director for Certification, Division of Teacher Education and Certification, Raleigh, January 12, 1971.

Taylor, Raymond M. Marshal and Librarian 6f the Supreme Court of North Carolina, Raleigh, January 11, 1973.

Triplett, Suzanne. Program Consultant for Research and Evaluation, Learning Institute of North Carolina, Durham, February 27, 1973.

Woodson, Ruth. Consultant, Division of Kindergarten-Early Childhood Education, State Department of Public Instruction, Raleigh, January 12, 1973.

Letters

Abrams, W. Amos. Former editor of North Carolina Education, March 1, 1971; March 20, 1971.

Aldrich, Harold L. Vice-President, National Kindergarten Association, Naples, Florida, August 23, 1971.

Association for Childhood Education International, August 13, 1971.

Ballentine, Rebecca S. Librarian, Institute of Government, Chapel Hill, February 10, 1972.

Barnes, Charlotte. Kindergarten Supervisor for the State Department of Public Instruction, October 20, 1971.

Brown, William J., Jr. Director of Research and Information Center, State Department of Public Insturction, April 23, 1971.

Carroll, Charles F. Former State Superintendent of Public Instruction, April 13, 1971.

Comfort, Elizabeth. Reference Librarian, State Historical Society of Missouri, Columbia, Missouri, October 9, 1971.

Crevar, Barbara. Retrieval Specialist, Research and Information Center, State Department of Public Instruction, October 4, 1971.

Day, Barbara. Early Childhood Education, University of North Carolina, Chapel Hill, March 20, 1971.

Evans, Martha. Former Senator from Mecklenburg County, August 9, 1971.

Gilmore, Voit. Former Senator from Guilford County, August 9, 1971.

Hodges, Luther. Former Governor of North Carolina, August 18, 1971.

Hunter, Eugenia. Professor of Education Emeritus, University of North Carolina, Greensboro, March 20, 1971.

Jenkins, James W. Director of Division of Kindergarten-Early Childhood Education, State Department of Public Instruction, March 20, 1971.

Landsberger, Betty. Learning Institute of North Carolina, March 20, 1971.

Loflin, Emily. Historian for Beaufort, North Carolina, October 11, 1971.

Maynard, William R. Research and Public Relations Assistant, North Carolina Association of Educators, August 26, 1971.

Montague, Patsy. Former Elementary Supervisor for the State Department of Public Instruction, March 13, 1971.

Moore, Dan. Former Governor of North Carolina, August 18, 1971.

Murray, Annie Mae. Professor of Education Emeritus, East Carolina University, March 18, 1971; June 19, 1972.

Peet, Mrs. Creighton. Executive Director, National Kindergarten Association, August 26, 1971.

Ray, Richard. Director of the Learning Institute of North Carolina, April 19, 1971.

Sanders, John. Director, Institute of Government, Chapel Hill, August 26, 1971.

Scott, Robert W. Governor of North Carolina, June 2, 1972.

Talley, J.W. Superintendent of Roanoke Rapids Graded School
District, January 8, 1971.

Taylor, J. Arthur. Assistant Director of Certification,
State Department of Public Instruction, March 20, 1971.

Vanore, Andrew. Deputy Attorney General of North Carolina,
August 5, 1971.

Wetherington, Julia. Former Elementary Supervisor with the
State Department of Public Instruction, May 1, 1971.

Catalogues and Pamphlets

Annual Report of Asheville Free Kindergarten Association for
1903-04. Pamphlet without pagination, found in Minutes
of the Meetings of the School Committee, January, 1906-
June 22, 1909.

Association for Childhood Education International. History
of the Kindergarten Movement in the Southeastern States
and Delaware, District of Columbia, New Jersey and
Pennsylvania. Atlanta, Ga.: Association for Childhood
Education International, 1939.

_____. The Kindergarten Centennial 1837-1937. Washington,
D. C.: Association for Childhood Education International,
1937.

Beaufort Kindergarten Training School. Kindergarten Normal
Department, St. Paul's School. Beaufort: Printing
Department of St. Paul's School, n.d.

Born A-Growing. A Summary Report of the North Carolina
Comprehensive School Improvement Project, 1964-1967.
Raleigh: State Department of Public Instruction,
November, 1968.

Bureau of Education. Kindergartens in the United States.
Bulletin #6, 1914.

Catalogues of East Carolina Teachers College, 1912-1915,
1921-1948.

Catalogues of the Trustees, Visitors, Faculty and Students
of Normal College, Randolph County, North Carolina,
1850-1855.

Catalogues of the University of North Carolina at Chapel Hill, 1878-1905.

Circular and Catalogue of the Trustees, Instructors and Pupils of Peace Institute for Young Ladies. Raleigh, North Carolina: Uzzell and Wiley, Printers and Binders, 1880-1890.

Criner, Beatrice H., ed. Directions for Title I. State Administration, Title I, ESEA, 1969.

_____. Off the Record, ESEA in 1967-1968. Raleigh: State Department of Public Instruction, Title I, ESEA, 1969.

Education Directory, Public School Systems, 1970-71. U.S. Government Printing Office, 1971.

"Head Start in the Public Schools, 1966-67," National Education Association Research Bulletin, XLVI (March, 1968), 3-8.

Institute of Government. Daily Legislative Bulletin. Chapel Hill: Institute of Government, 1963, 1965, 1967, 1969.

"Kindergarten Education, 1967-68," National Education Association Research Bulletin, XLVII (March, 1969), 10-13.

State Department of Public Instruction. The Kindergarten in North Carolina. Raleigh: State Department of Public Instruction, June, 1953. Publication No. 294.

_____. Rationale, Goals, and Plans for the Improvement of Education in North Carolina. Raleigh: State Department of Public Instruction, 1970.

_____. Schools for Young Children. Raleigh, North Carolina: State Superintendent of Public Instruction, 1955.

_____. Teaching in North Carolina. Raleigh: State Department of Public Instruction, October, 1969.

Letter, E. C. Brooks to Bessie Locke, July 14, 1921.
North Carolina Department of Archives and History,
Letter File, Office of the Superintendent of Public
Instruction, Box 32.

Letter, G. P. Carr to Charles F. Carroll, February 9, 1962,
Research and Information Center, State Department of
Public Instruction.

Letter, Bessie Locke to E. C. Brooks, June 21, 1921. North
Carolina Department of Archives and History, Letter
File, Office of the Superintendent of Public Instruction,
Box 32.

Letter, Ralph Moody, Assistant Attorney General, to Superintendent G. P. Carr, February 23, 1962, Research and
Information Center, State Department of Public Instruction.

Letter, Anne Rabe to Superintendent Clyde Erwin, May 10, 1941,
North Carolina Department of Archives and History, Letter
File, Office of the Superintendent of Public Instruction,
Box 32.

Letter, Hattie M. Scott to E. E. Sams, October 10, 1913,
North Carolina Department of Archives and History,
Letter File, Office of Superintendent of Public
Instruction, Box 32.

Letter, Nina C. Vandewalker to E. C. Brooks, July 14, 1921,
North Carolina Department of Archives and History,
Letter File, Office of the Superintendent of Public
Instruction, Box 32.

Manuscripts Department, William R. Perkins Library, Papers of
Braxton Craven, Duke University.

Law Reports

Posey et al. v. Board of Education of Buncombe County et al.,
199 N.C., 306-314.

"Submission of Controversy Without Action," in Robert E. Posey
et al. v. Board of Education of Buncombe County et al.,
in the Supreme Court of North Carolina, Buncombe County,
No. 607J (1930).